Get Your Child Ready for an IQ Test

and for Gifted Child Qualification Process

by

The L.I.B Child Development Association

Table of Content

Introduction

IQ, Intelligence Quotient, is a score that reflects how "smart" a person is compared to others when measured by a particular test or set of challenges. As long as you do not over-interpret IQ, well-designed and standardized intelligence tests are among the most accurate of all psychological tests and assessments.

The standard IQ test was created to evaluate children between the ages of 5 and 16 who are functioning within a broad range of cognitive development. These tests are used in various cases, when a parent or a certain institute wants to get a more objective evaluation of the child's intellectual abilities. In a typical scenario a child will have to be evaluated against other children, for example when applying to special education programs, to a specific school or as part of a gifted children program qualification process.

An IQ test for children consists of various tasks that measure short-term memory, analytical thinking, mathematical ability and spatial recognition. Like all IQ tests the main goal is not to measure the amount of information a child has accumulated, but rather their capacity to learn. However, in most tests the ability to learn is tested based on the assumption that the child already has a certain level of knowledge. Moreover, especially in tests that aim to identify gifted children, significant weight is given to general knowledge measuring.

Why Prepare?

You know your child and you recognize that their ability is way above average, so you assume that the IQ or any other admission test will reflect this fact. Well, you are only half right. You must get your child ready for two main reasons:

- Practicing and leaning various techniques improves the score by 10%-25%
- In many cases your child is competing against other children, especially if the score is required or reviewed as part of an evaluation or admission process. It doesn't matter how smart your child is, their score must be higher than the others.

So in order to give your child a fair chance and avoid disappointment, you must let them practice and learn how to answer the different tests in a quick and accurate way. In this book you will get the tools that will enable your child to fulfill their full potential and get the most out of the test.

A short preparation, a few hours per week in the couple of weeks before the tests, will improve your child's knowledge and mental readiness dramatically

How to Prepare?

We provide you with the tools to help your child prepare. The preparation is divided into three parts: general strategies and tips, ideas for additional activities that can assist the preparation, and of course example tests.

Your role, as a parent, is to be your child's mentor. Read the instructions and understand them, then read them again with your child, making sure they understand the rules and the examples. Then let them practice on their own, one test at a time. When done, go through each test together and review both the correct answers and the wrong answers, ensuring the child knows the right way to address each of the questions. As you can see, you have a lot of responsibility. Note that it's okay to find some of the questions difficult; not all are trivial. However, you should be able to show your child that you are willing to make the effort and try to solve each and every question.

What is the Meaning of the IQ Score?

After you get back the IQ test results you will probably ask yourself what the score means. Is your child gifted? If so, how gifted?

Before you can understand what it means for a child to be gifted, you need to understand what IQ scores represent. An IQ score is an Intelligence Quotient, which is a measure of intelligence, primarily reasoning ability. The higher the score, the greater the reasoning ability.

If we took everyone's IQ scores and plotted them, we would see that they would be distributed in a normal bell curve. That means that most scores would fall somewhere in the center of that bell curve. The score in the absolute center of the bell curve is 100 (IQ score of 100) and that is where we would expect most scores to fall, or where we expect them to cluster.

As the scores move away from the norm (100), we will find fewer and fewer scores. However, to make the numbers meaningful, we need to be able to measure the variability of the scores.

Once you understand these scores and how they fit in a bell curve, you can better understand the different categories of giftedness. Why is a score between 115 and 130 considered mildly gifted? Why is a score of 131 and 145 highly gifted? The answer lies in the standard deviation of the scatter of IQ scores on the bell curve. The standard deviation used in many tests, including the Weschsler IQ test, is 15. The majority of test scores (about 70%) fall somewhere between one standard deviation below and one standard deviation above 100. This means that most scores are somewhere between 85 and 115. Those scores are considered the "average" or normal intelligence range.

The farther the score is from 100, the fewer people we will find with that score. If we move one additional standard deviation below and one additional standard deviation above 100, we will find about 25% of the scores falling within those ranges. In other words, people with IQs between 70 and 85 and between 115 and 130 make up about 25% of the population. That leaves only about 5% of the population who will have scores somewhere beyond those first two standard deviations away from the norm.

In most cases the IQ scores are translated into the following categories:

- Mildly Gifted – IQ score between 115 to 129
- Moderately Gifted – IQ score between 130 to 144
- Highly Gifted – IQ score between 145 to 159
- Exceptionally Gifted – IQ score between 160 to 179
- Profoundly Gifted – IQ score over 180

IQ testing is not a science. It may seem that way at times, but it's not. Scores from tests are really estimates based on test performance on a particular day. There is always a margin of error. However, it is also important to note that the score does represent ability. That is, a child who gets a score of 140 did not get that score because he or she had a "good day". Some people may tell parents that about their children, but it's not true. The highest score a child gets will be the best reflection of the child's IQ (within the margin of error). An average child cannot get a score that high just because they ate a good breakfast and felt good that day!

The other direction however is valid: A "bad day" will for sure take the score down. We cannot always control our child's health condition, but we can control many other aspects that may lead to a "bad day", mainly wrong attitude and lack of preparation. A child that feels confident, that knows what is expected of them and understands the importance of the test will be less likely to have a "bad day" during the test.

Getting Ready

General Tips for Success

Most IQ tests are multiple choice tests, in which the examinee needs to choose one correct answer out of several options. It's important that the child understands the implications of such a test, positive and negative. The answers are sometimes confusing, providing more than one option that seems to be correct. The child must understand that he must select one answer, the one that is the most accurate. This is done by reviewing all answers before selecting one. Many children, mostly the clever ones, tend to cut corners; if they find an answer that seems to be correct they will mark it and move on to the next question. This method will fail them in an IQ test, as many times almost correct answers are provided in order to confuse and slow down the examinees. So, tell your child to read through the answer and select the most suitable one. If the right answer is not evident, an educated guess process should be applied:

- Disqualified wrong answers. Even if the right answer is not clearly identified, some answers can easily be qualified as wrong. These answers should be rolled out in order to ease the selection of the right one.
- Use grammar rules (for verbal tests) - See if the answer wording and grammatical rule matches the question: the wording, tense, gender, plural/singular etc.
- Use intuition and guess. It's better to guess and not leave a question unanswered.
- Marked guessed questions and if time permits get back to them at the end. Sometimes a clear look helps with identifying the right answer.

IQ tests are created so almost all examinees will not be able to complete the tests. This is required in order to allow quick thinkers with natural intuition or broad knowledge to get higher scores. It's important that you guide your child to use the available time efficiently:

- Do not waste time. It seems trivial but many children fail to understand the importance of that.
  - Start each section of the test as soon as possible.
  - Do not ask questions during the test itself, just before or after each section.
  - Do not spend too much time on each question. If the answer is not clear, mark the question and get back to it at the end as explained before.
  - Do not spend time on anything else but the test itself. I've seen children that draw pictures, mess with their pens or just daydream.
- Although the time is short, instruct your child not to take shortcuts.
  - All questions and answers must be thoroughly read.
  - The instruction must be understood (if written in the test itself). The child may assume that they are familiar with instructions as the test is similar to one of the tests they have practiced before. Although this will probably be the case, the actual test may still be different than the example practice tests.
- When the time of a specific section is almost over usually the examiner will announce it, or in the case of a computer-based test the timer will indicate that the remaining time is short (e.g. 30 seconds). This is the time to guess and mark answers for all skipped and remaining questions.

Children, mainly the clever ones, tend to overlook the obvious and miss the sometimes straightforward answers. It's important that the child is aware of this and will know that the tests will not include tricky or devious questions. The questions, although sometimes difficult, will not be unfair and will not require a twisted deduction route. Usually the obvious understanding of the question and the straightforward answer are the right ones.

And last but not least, you should not over-pressure your child. The whole preparation process should be regarded as fun, quality parent-child time. The child should be encouraged, even if not always successful. Most children will actually enjoy most of the preparation tests. You know your child, so you should know just how much pressure should be applied and when; just remember that over-pressuring may lead to motivation loss, which will affect the preparation process and the test itself.

Test Structure

There is no one standard format used in all cases. The structure and length are defined per case. Normally younger children will have shorter tests, different institutes focus on different capabilities, and periodical changes in all aspects are made in order to ensure that information about the test will not be improperly used and so on. However, the underlying knowledge and fundamental knowhow required to better perform in such tests remains the same.

IQ, cognitive and intelligence tests will normally include a few sections, sub-tests, of different types. In the next section we will outline the different types of tests and provide examples.

Note that not all types of sub-tests will always appear. Each institution selects a few types of sub-tests in order to create the full test. Changes in the tests are also expected in order to prevent examinees from sharing information about the test with others. Nevertheless, this book is designed to address the challenges and to provide your child with the knowledge and tools to cope with differently structured tests.

Answer Selection

In most cases the tests will not be performed using a computer. The examined will get the text notebook and optionally a separate paper on which the answers should be marked. Although it seems trivial, children sometimes find it hard to understand the way in which the answers should be marked and what to do in case a previous answer selection needs to be changed.

First, instruct your child to listen carefully when the tester explains the required procedure, and encourage them to ask in case the explanation was not clear. In some cases the only explanation is a short text that the child needs to read and understand on their own. Also, in such cases the child will usually have the option to ask for additional explanations.

Last, please read the instruction you got prior to the test carefully. In most cases you will be instructed to equip your child with blue or black pen; in others you will be requested to bring a pencil and an eraser. Do not ignore these instructions!

Below you will see the most common methods for answer selection and marking for non-computerized tests.

Answering on the Text Form Itself
In this case the examinee selects an answer by circling it, its number or its letter. For example:

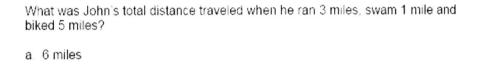

What was John's total distance traveled when he ran 3 miles, swam 1 mile and biked 5 miles?

a   6 miles

b   7 miles

c   8 miles

d   9 miles

In case the examinee changed their mind, and decided to select another answer, they will need to x-cross the marked circle on the former answer. For example:

What was John's total distance traveled when he ran 3 miles, swam 1 mile and biked 5 miles?

a   6 miles

b   7 miles

c   8 miles

9 miles

It is OK to change the answer again, even back to the previously x-crossed answer. For example:

What was John's total distance traveled when he ran 3 miles, swam 1 mile and biked 5 miles?

a   6 miles

b   7 miles

8 miles

9 miles

Answering on a Separate Sheet

An additional sheet of paper may be provided just to mark the answers on. The method is similar to the method explained before, for example:

Test 5 - General Knowladge

Test 6 - Math

1. a b c d
2. a b c d
3. a b c d

Answering Using an Answers Card

Another common method is an Answers Card. These cards are used by large organizations and aimed to be processed by optical card readers. These cards are usually filled in with a pencil, not a pen, and the way to correct an answer is to erase the previous marking before marking a new answer.

The Answers Cards are mechanically read by sensitive optical devices, and each random marking or dirt on the card my cause wrong results. In order to avoid this the following simple rules should be applied:

- Use the correct pencil, as instructed beforehand (e.g. 2B pencil).
- Do not apply too much pressure on the card while marking an answer, as later on it will be difficult to make a change.
- When erasing a mark, ensure that it was completely removed and other questions' markings were not accidently deleted.

In all cases the marking is performed by filling in the desired answer area on the card. In some cases the child will be instructed to completely fill in the area, while in other cases a simple line through the area will be sufficient, for example:

Below you will find a few example cards:

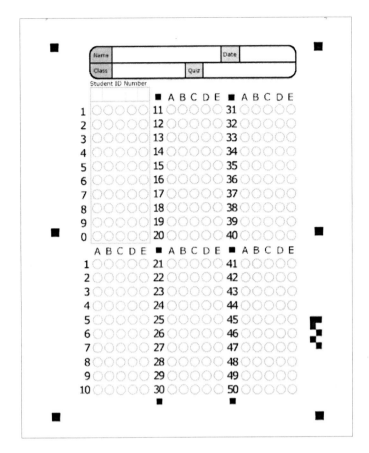

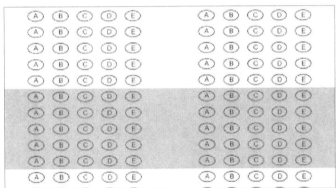

Get your child ready for an IQ test

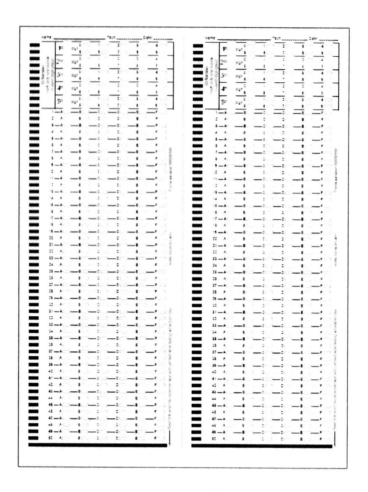

Types of Tests

As mentioned before, IQ, cognitive and intelligence tests will normally include a few sub-tests of different types. In this section we will outline the different types of tests, review the different tests available in each category, provide examples and explain how each test should be addressed. Note that not all types of sub-tests will always appear. The next section includes example tests, of all different types, to be used for self practice.

General Knowledge

These tests measure the level of general knowledge in many domains. Usually the tests will be composed of about ten questions covering different areas. The questions will be followed by several answers from which the child should select the most appropriate one, for example:

Paris is the capital city of:
> A. London
> B. France
> C. Spain
> D. Portugal

Obviously the right answer is: **B. France.**

The practice tests below cover a wide variety of knowledge, however it is important to practice beyond these tests: encourage the child to read, play trivia games, watch the news and documentaries together and initiate discussions around relevant topics. The list below covers the domains that usually appear in the tests:
- Contemporary local and world politics (presidents, constitution etc.)
- Current events - Prominent events in the news in recent months, for example wars and disputes, natural disasters.
- Religion
- Geography - Continents, neighboring countries, mountains, oceans, compass directions.
- Astronomy - Solar System, astronomical phenomena like solar and lunar eclipses.
- Biology - Parts of the flower, types of animals (e.g. a fish is not a mammal).
- Famous inventors
- Famous writers and composers
- Famous people - Nobel Prize winners, poets and writers, famous athletes, founders of the nation.
- Units of measurement:
  - Temperature: degrees Celsius and Fahrenheit
  - Length: Metric and inches
  - Basic engineering: length, perimeter, volume, and surface area
  - Weight: grams and kilograms, pounds and ounces
  - Volume: gallons, liters
  - Speed: miles per hour, meters per second
  - Time: seconds, minutes, hours, days, weeks, months
- Prices: Dollars and cents, other currencies

Vocabulary and Verbal Comprehension Tests

There are several types of tests that aim to evaluate children's vocabulary and verbal compression. We will present below the three common tests that are normally used for this purpose.

In addition to getting the child familiar with these tests and providing a proper practice, it is important to enrich children's vocabulary and sharpen their understanding of the following areas:

- What is a synonym and what is just a similar word? Synonyms must describe exactly the same, and have exactly the same meaning.
- What is an antonym? An antonym must have a meaning which must provide an opposite meaning to the original word.
- What is an exceptional word and how do you recognize a word or an unusual concept in a list of words?

You can enrich your child's knowledge in fun ways like word games and puzzles. Driving time for example can be exploited to enrich the vocabulary via games:

- Synonyms Game: One person says a word and the others have to find as many synonyms for the word. It's important that as many as possible will join the game and say their words as well so the child will learn from the others.
- Antonyms Game: Same as before, one says a word and the others have to find as many antonyms as possible.
- Guess Words: The parent or an older sibling says a word that the child does not know. The child should try to guess the meaning.

Including the possibility of guessing the meaning of an unfamiliar word is important and may help with success in these types of tests. Words' meanings can be guessed by trying to identify the word's root, by asking questions like: what does it sound like? What does it remind you of? Children who learn this ability will be able to better deal with the various questions that appear in these sections of the test.

These are the four common types of questions in this domain:

Synonyms

In these questions the examinee is presented with words (or short terms) followed by several possible interpretations. The examinee should choose the most appropriate options. For example:

Which of the following is a synonym for the word **Dispatch**?
- A. Communication
- B. Tag
- C. Hesitation
- D. Speedy

The correct answer is "communication".

The difficulty in this part of the test is twofold: first the child should recognize or understand the word and the interpretations, and then choose the most appropriate interpretation out of often confusing or misleading options.

Antonyms
This test questions also include a word and a number of options. Here the examinee needs to choose the word's antonym, the word with an opposite meaning. For example:

Shallow
      A. Water
      B. Dry
      C. Deep
      D. Low

The correct answer is of course "Deep".

Here, too, a child who does not recognize all the words will find it difficult to answer correctly. The recommendation here is to instruct your child to take the following steps:

- If at least one of the options is recognized and it means the opposite – do not hesitate to mark it as the correct answer.
- If three of the four options are known and none seems to be the right answer, the fourth option is probably the right one.
- Otherwise, try to figure out the meaning of the words as explained above, by the way the sound, even by trying to say them out loud. In many cases the child will think of something but will not be sure, and this is when intuition should be followed.
- If none of these help, just make a guess and move on.

Odd One Out
This test presents a number of options (four options usually). The examinee shall indicate which of the words or terms is an exception; which does not belong to the group all the other options do. For example:

Driver, Watchmaker, Shoemaker, Person

The correct answer is obviously "Person". All other words describe professions.

Another example:

Plane, Bird, Rocket, Dog

The correct answer is "Dog". All other words belongs to the group: things that can fly.

In this test the words are usually simple and familiar, as the main goal is to test the ability to identify relationships and word meanings. It is important to practice the ability to identify a common theme for a number of words. Beyond solving the sample tests below, you can play a game called Packages:

- One participant, "the packer" in this turn, chooses a theme (and doesn't tell the others yet). For example: fruits.
- Now the packer chooses a word that belongs to the theme, for example: orange, and says aloud: I'm packaging "orange"
- The others, in turn, try to guess what the theme is. They should not say the theme itself but look for another word that fits the theme.
    - In this example one can think that the theme is colors, and say: I'm packaging "green". In this case the packer will say: "get out" and the turn moves to the next one.
    - The next may think that the theme is fruits and say: I'm packaging "banana". Since this matches the selected theme the packer will say: "packed".
- This continues until all are "packed", or all give up.

This is a great game that helps expand one's vocabulary and ability to classify words and terms into themes. You can use the list of topics above in the General Knowledge section as a list of possible themes.

Missing Words (Sentence Completion)

In this verbal test the examinee is presented with sentences. Each sentence is missing a word. The examinee shall select from four options the most appropriate word to complete the sentence. For example:

The ball _____ on the floor.

- Basketball
- Jump
- Bounces
- Dances

In this case the correct answer is "bounces". Although some of the other options have a similar meaning, they are less suitable to describe the bouncing ball. The word should also be syntactically correct and the grammar roles must be followed, so in this case for example the word "jump" is not a valid match.

As with the word interpretation test, the child should be instructed to try and guess if none or some of the words are unknown. If the child knows only some of the words, the words that do not match can be ruled out, allowing them to focus on the options that are familiar. Also, here it should be possible to guess based on the root of the word. Another way is to try and embed the word in the sentence and see whether it sounds right and meaningful:

- Is the singular or plural form correct?
- What type of word is expected? A verb or a noun? An action (bouncing ball) or a description (tall girl)? A quantity (most students) or a relation (he is bigger than)? A cause (because of being late) or the opposite (negation: despite being late)?

Beyond the practice sample tests also here, the best way to prepare for these questions is to enrich children's vocabulary as previously described.

Conceptual Relations

A large portion of many IQ tests is devoted to the recognition and utilization of different types of connections and sometimes abstract relations between words, images, symbols and shapes. This part requires learning the rules listed below and a lot of practice. Most children find this part difficult, at least initially, but after experiencing the sample test the results significantly improve.

In addition to the practice the sample test provides, you may purchase one or two of the many board or online games that require the child to find connections and analogies between elements of different kinds.

There are three main types of such tests: verbal, visual and configurational. These three types are detailed below:

Verbal Relations

In this sub-test the examinee needs to identify the relationship between words, and apply the same relationship to another word. In most cases three words will be presented, and a list of words from which the answer should be selected. The examinee will have to understand how the first two words relate to each other, and then find the word that will relate to the third word in a similar way. These questions require the child to also recognize the words and understand the context. For example:

Clock : Time | Thermometer : _____

Norse, Temperature, Sick, Doctor

The answer is **Temperature**. Clock is used for measuring the time and a thermometer is used for measuring the temperature. Other answers may be confusing as the child can find a relation between them and the third word (e.g. The Norse is using a Thermometer), however if this is not the same relation that the first two words have, it is not the right answer.

A good way to make sure that the chosen answer is correct is to formulate a sentence that expresses the relation between the first two words and try to use the same sentence with the third word and candidate answer. For example: "A clock is a device that measures the time", "A thermometer is a device that measures the temperature". In this way we can validate that the answer is correct or disqualifies incorrect answers, for example: "A thermometer is a device that measures the doctor" is not a logical statement and therefore is incorrect.

The following table outlines some of the most common verbal relationships. Learning these roles and examples will help with getting the right answers quickly and accurately:

Relations	Examples	
Levels of magnetite	Large : Enormous	Small : Tiny
Opposites	High : Low	Winter : Summer
Identities	High: Tall	Earth : The World
Items and their group	Spring : Seasons	January : Months
Belongs to the same group	January : May	Spring : Winter Truck: Motorcycle
Part of...	Hand : Clock	Wheel : Automobile
Used for...	Glass : Drinking	Boat : Sailing
Type of...	Fork : Cutlery	Shirt : Clothing
Characteristic of...	Summer : Warm	Grass : Green
Action and effect	Sewing : Shirt	Joke : Laughter
Old and new	Wagon : Car	Abacus : Calculator

Visual Relations

This test is similar to the Verbal Relations test that was presented in the previous section, however instead of using written words, the relations are presented as images.

As before, three images are presented followed by a list of images from which the answer should be selected. The first two images relate to each other and represent a relation. The examinee needs to find out, from the list of options the image that creates, together with the third image, the same relation that exists between the first two images. For example:

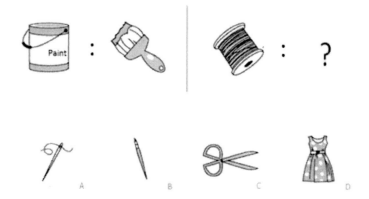

The correct answer is A - a needle. Here, too, the best way to make sure that the chosen answer is correct is to formulate a sentence that expresses the relation between the first two pictures and find the image that has the same relation with the same image. For example: "to use paint you will need a brush", "to use a sewing thread you will need a needle". This method helps the examinee to validate or disqualify answers in a fast and accurate way.

Although it seems similar, some of the visual relations tests include configurative relations questions. These questions require and measure different skills. Also, in this case the examinee is presented with one relation, and according to it the answer that formulates the same relation should be selected. However, the relations here are not verbal or conceptual, they are spatial and geometric. For example:

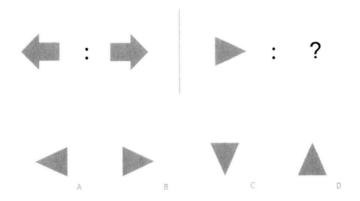

The correct answer is A, as the relation is "mirroring". The next section explains more about these types of relations and the way to identify them.

Shapes

Shape Inclusion

This test assesses the child's ability to identify figures and isolate a part of a shape or pattern. A simple shape is presented on the left-hand side, followed by a sequence of more complex shapes. The examinee should select a complex shape that precisely includes the simple one: all of it, in the same size and in the same orientation. For example:

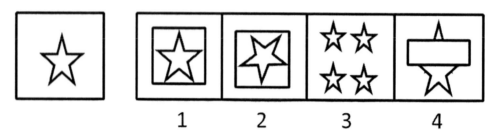

The right answer is 1, as only this shape includes the shape on the left as is: complete, same size and same orientation.

Mirror Image

This test checks the child's figurative and special perception. A mirror image of a figure is an image that is identical in form but with the structure reversed, as in a mirror: reflected duplication of the original figure that appears identical but reversed. The following example shows a pair of an image and its mirror image:

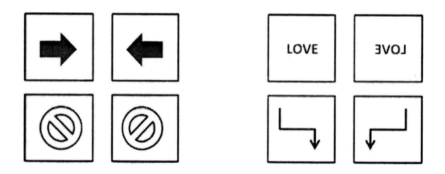

In the text, the examinee is presented with an image and out of several options selects its mirror image.

Paper Folding

The paper folding questions are similar in concept to the standard image mirroring questions and require similar cognitive skills. However, the questions are more difficult and most children find them very challenging.

Also, here a pattern is given followed by four alternatives to its right. The pattern is seemingly printed on a transparent sheet. The examinee needs to select the one image on the right that shows how the pattern would appear when the transparent sheet is folded at the dotted line. For example:

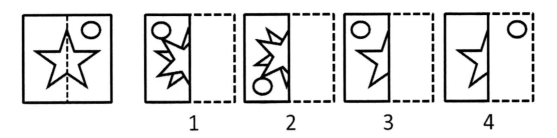

1   2   3   4

The correct answer is 3.

Why?

The star is symmetric, so if we fold it at the dotted line the folded half will unite with the non-folded part:

The circle which resides on the right section will move to the left after the folding:

Sequence of Shapes

This test evaluates the child's spatial perception and pattern recognition capabilities. A sequence of shapes is presented and the examinee should select a shape that continues the sequence while keeping the same transition logic and shape pattern rules. For example:

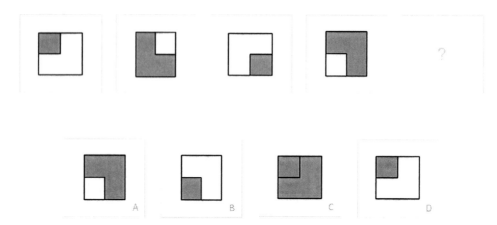

The sequence of shapes shown above use two rules in the transition from one shape to the next:

- The whole shape is rotated ninety degrees clockwise
- The colors are alternating:
  - The color of the inner square is changing from gray to white or from white to gray
  - The color of the outer square is also changing from gray to white or from white to gray

Therefore the correct answer is A as it is the only shape that keeps both rules.

The transitions rules can be expressed in several ways. The table below illustrates the transition rules that may appear in these types of questions (obviously several of these rules may be applied together in a single transition):

Transition Rule	The whole shape	Part of the shape
Rotation, clockwise or counter clockwise		
Mirror image		
Coloring		
Internal order of elements	Irrelevant	
Addition or deduction of elements		
Augmentation or reduction		

Arithmetic Word Problems

These tests examine arithmetical capabilities together with reading comprehension. Although most children face similar questions in school, most children find this part difficult, and the highest number of errors is found in these tests.

The problems are presented in a verbal manner. The child must fully understand the question and identify the various arithmetical components in order to calculate the answer:

- Given numerical data (e.g. **Danny has 5 balloons** - **5** is given)
- The arithmetical relation between the given data elements (e.g. **Janet has 3 balloons more than Danny** - the arithmetical relation is **addition of three**)
- The arithmetical actions need to be executed in order to complete the missing data (Janet's number of balloons is 8. **5 + 3 = 8**)
- The solution to the question (e.g. **How many balloons do Janet and Danny have together?** With the data identified and calculated earlier, the problem can be answered: in total they both have 8 + 5 = **13 balloons**)

Common question types relate to periods of time: minutes in an hour, hours in a day, days in a week and months in a year. Another type of question deals with currency and prices: dollars and cents. It is important to practice these time measurements with your child. For example:

- How many hours of sleep did John have if he went to bed at nine o'clock in the evening and woke up at six thirty in the morning?
- How long is a TV show that starts at 3:54PM and ends at 5:11PM?
- The vacation starts on Thursday and ends on Tuesday. For how many days will school be closed?
- A popsicle costs two dollars and 60 cents, how much do two popsicles cost? How much change will you get from a 10 dollar bill?

The following example illustrates a more complex problem that requires a higher level of arithmetic deduction skills and more complex calculations:

Adam inflated balloons for his birthday party. He inflated 16 red balloons, 22 green balloons, and twice the number of blue balloons. How many balloons will Adam have for his party?

The given data is the number of red balloons (16) and green balloons (22).
The number of blue balloons is missing, but it can calculated using the fact that it is double the number of green balloons (i.e. 22 + 22 = 44 or 22 x 2 = 44).
Now the required answer, the total number of balloons, can be calculated:
16 + 22 + 44 = 82 balloons.

The problems are usually based on addition or subtraction of numbers between 1 to 100. Most of the problems can be solved without the direct use of multiplication and division, but children who know how to use it will be able to answer the questions much more quickly, thus gaining a higher score by accomplishing more accurate results. Memorizing the multiplication table is therefore highly recommended.

Starting from the 2nd or 3rd grade, problems that involve fractions may also appear. The children should at least be aware of the following:

- What does a fraction represent? What does the numerator and denominator stand for? (e.g. a pizza is divided into 8 slices. If you ate 3 slices you ate $\frac{3}{8}$ of the pizza.)
- How are fractions written?
- Sizes of fragments (e.g. half bigger than a quarter).
- Basic operations with basic fractions: half, quarter and third.

Last but not least, explain to the child that drafts can and should be used. Writing down all given data, intermediate results and the way the answer is constructed can help them avoid mistakes.

Series

Series questions usually appear in tests aimed for age 10 and up. However, since in rare cases such questions have appeared in younger children's tests, we recommend that all children at all ages practice it as well, or at least understand the way in which such questions should be addressed.

Numerical Series Completion

The numerical series completion questions examine logical reasoning together with arithmetical abilities. The child is required to apply their arithmetical knowledge in order to identify logic and patterns, and based on that deduct the next missing item of the presented series. These tests usually include several levels of questions, from basic simple series to series which are structured from several patterns warped together.

Many children will find this part difficult at first, but after practicing and learning to identify the conventional patterns this type of question become less intimidating. In addition to practicing using the sample tests, it's important that the child is aware of their mistakes, and get an explanation on the right way to answer.

The following examples show different numerical series, and present the most common solving strategies:

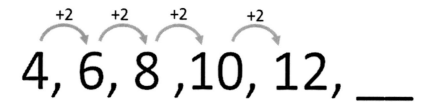

In this series the relation between each pair of consecutive numbers is the addition of two. Based on that we can conclude that in order to calculate the missing number we need to add two to the number before it:
$12 + 2 = 14$
The answer is: 14

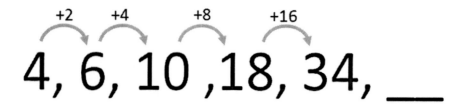

Also in this series there is an 'addition' relation between each pair of consecutive numbers. The relation however is more complex, taking into account the previous relation and doubles the number that needs to be added in each step:

2
$2 \times 2 = 4$
$4 \times 2 = 8$
$8 \times 2 = 16$

Applying the same logic to the last available number in the series will allow us to calculate the missing number:
$34 + (16 \times 2. = 34 + 32 = 66$
The answer is: 66

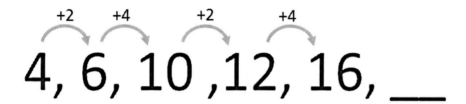

This series includes two different patterns: an addition of two and an addition of four alternately. Therefore, in order to calculate the next number in the series we need to add two to the last available number: $16 + 2 = 18$
The answer is: 18
(By the way, the following number in the series will be 22, do you understand why?)

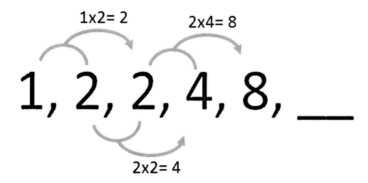

The last example shows a different pattern. Starting from the third number, each number in the series is the result of the multiplication of the two numbers before it.
The missing number will therefore be the multiplication of 4 and 8: $4 \times 8 = 32$
The answer is: 32

Sequence of Letters

In this test, the examinee should recognize a pattern in a sequence of letters. The patterns are usually simple, however the child will have to transform the letters into numbers in order to identify it. There are several variations, but usually the examinee will be presented with four sequences of letters, where three of them use the same pattern and one doesn't. The child will first have to figure out the pattern of each sequence and then identify the sequence that uses a different pattern than the others. Example:

1. CDCDC
2. MNMNM
3. XZXZX
4. EFEFE

In this case the exceptional sequence is number 3. The other sequences use the same pattern: a letter, the next letter in the alphabet, the first letter again and so on. The 3rd sequence however uses a different pattern: the second letter in a pair is not the consequent letter but the next letter in the alphabet

The patterns will always be based on the location of the letters in the alphabet. It is important that the child can recognize the alphabet and its order.

The table below contains examples of patterns that may appear in the tests:

Pattern Logic	Details	Examples
Ascending Order	Alphabetical order leaps	ABCDE BDFHJ
Descending Order	Counter alphabetical order leaps	EDCBA JHFDB
Skipping/Leaping	The leaps values are a numerical series of numbers with their own patter	ABDGK (1,2,3,4 letters leap) ABDHP (Doubled leap size)
Identical Leaps	Leap the same value back and forth	ACACA (+2, -2 … leaps) SPSPS (-3, +3 … leaps)
Non-Identical Leaps	Leap different value back and forth	ACADA (+2,-2,+3,-3 leaps) ADBEC (+3, -2 … leaps)
Single Leap	Only one leap in the whole sequence	AAEAA TTTOT

Some children may find it useful to mark, on the test form itself, the letter's alphabetical position or the value of the jump between each pair of letters in the sequence. This method can help them with identifying the patterns and avoiding mistakes; however, it is time-consuming and therefore not suited for every child. For example:

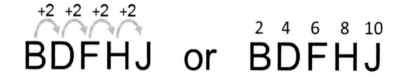

Raven's Matrices

The Raven's matrices test is the most common non-verbal multiple choice IQ test. It measures fluid intelligence: reasoning and problem-solving ability. Fluid intelligence is considered a core component of general intelligence. The test was initially considered to be 'culture fair'- unlike other tests that are affected by previous knowledge and learned skills, this test is supposed to measure fluid intelligence in a neutral objective manner. However, recent studies did show that people in different countries and with different backgrounds get different scores. Studies also showed that someone who is familiar with such tests will get a higher score than someone who has never experienced such a test before.

Each question in the test includes a 4×4, 3×3, or 2×2 matrix of elements. The examinee should identify the pattern of shapes in the matrix, and choose, out of six or eight options, the missing shape that will complete the matrix's pattern. The pattern can be identified by close inspection of the shapes in each row and column of the matrix.

For example:

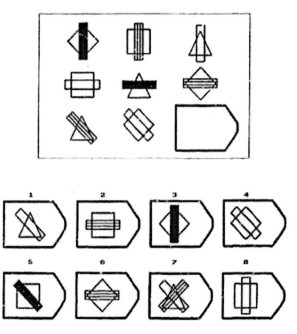

The correct answer is 5. The pattern and the shape logic in the rows and columns of this matrix can be defined by these three rules:

1. Each row contains 3 shapes (triangle, square, diamond).
2. Each row has 3 bars (black, striped, clear).
3. The orientation of each bar is the same within a row, but varies from row to row (vertical, horizontal, diagonal).

The only answer that applies to these three rules is answer number 5.

Five Rules for Matrices Problem Solving

John Raven, the test author, designed all the problems to be based on five basic types of rules. Each problem might have combinations of different rules or different instances of the same rule.

In order to solve the matrix's problems effectively, the child must understand and practice these rules:

1. **Constant in a row.** This is 'rule 3' in the matrix example above – the orientation of the bar is the same in each row, but changes down a column.

2. **Quantitative progression.** An increase or decrease between adjacent entries in size, position or number. An example of this rule is shown below:

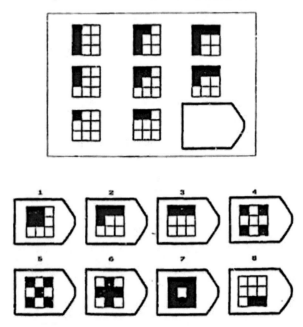

The correct answer is 3. The number of black squares in each entry increases in the top row from 1 to 2 to 3. Similarly, the number of black squares in the first column decreases from 3 to 2 to 1.

3. **Figure addition or subtraction.** A figure from one column is added to or subtracted from another column to produce the third. An example is given below (the correct answer is 8).

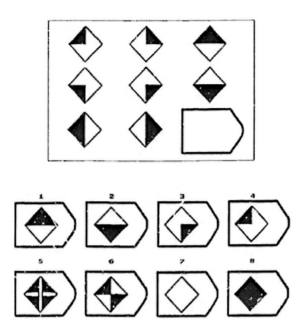

4. **Distribution of 3 values.** Three values of a category such as shape are always present in each row. Two examples of this rule are shown in the first matrix we looked at above. Each row contains 3 shapes (triangle, square, diamond), and each row has 3 bars (black, striped, clear).

5. **Distribution of 2 values.** Two values of a category such as shape are always present in each row, but the third is null/irrelevant. An example of this is given below.

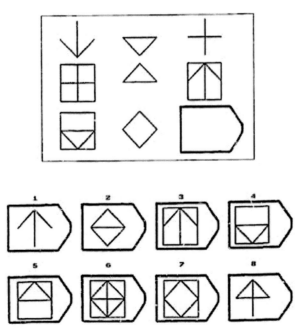

The correct answer is 5. Each figure element (horizontal line, vertical line, V shape) occurs two times in each row.

Corresponding Elements

In matrices problems with more complex patterns that include more than one rule, the examinee must figure out which elements in the matrix are governed by the same rule – something that can be called 'correspondence finding'.

An example of a correspondence problem is shown below:

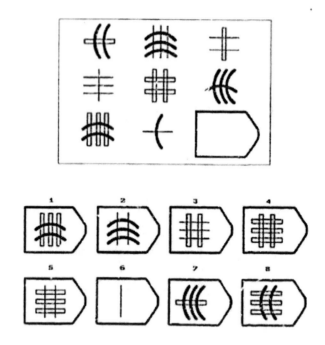

The correct answer is 5. Figuring out what corresponds to what requires that the examinee form a hypotheses in their mind, and tests this hypotheses out. A hypothesis is an imagined explanation or prediction that needs to be tested.

In the example above, one hypothesis is that one rule applies to the bars, another rule applies to the dark curves, and another rule applies to the straight lines. Although it's true that each row has two of each type of shape, this hypothesis doesn't explain the number or orientations of the different elements. Another hypothesis is needed. In the end it is orientation (vertical or horizontal) that is the basis of the rules needed to solve this problem. In each row there are always 1, 2 and 3 horizontal elements and 1, 2 and 3 vertical elements. In addition to this, 1, 2 and 3 elements of each shape are distributed across the three rows.

Note that such problems are difficult and intended for adult IQ tests. It is not likely that a child will encounter such problems in an IQ test; however, it is good to understand the hypotheses methodology and practice it.

Colors and Coloring Patterns Matrixes

Another type of matrices involves colors and coloring patterns instead of shapes' transitions and distribution.

These questions are considered easier and more suitable for children of primary school age, and therefore are likely to appear in the IQ and screening tests for children of all ages. There are no complex rules or reasoning flows to follow in this case. The only advice is to pay close attention to each question and to avoid reckless conclusions. The following examples illustrate these types of questions:

In the following example the correct answer is a 4. Answer 2 may be misleading to those who do not carefully examine all the possibilities.

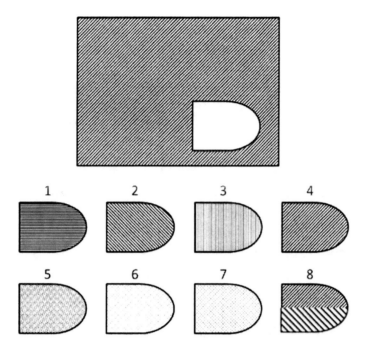

In the following example the correct answer is 6. Answer 7 may be misleading because it shows a similar texture, although is a bit more spacious.

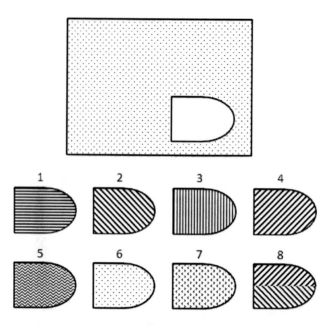

In the following example the correct answer is 8. Answers 1, 2, and 4 can be misleading.

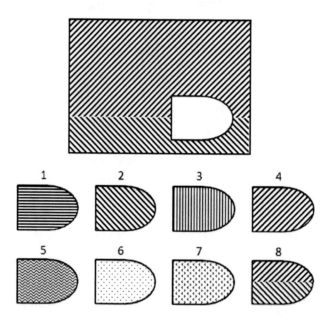

The following two examples demonstrate another type of repeating texture. However, the texture is not uniform and the direction, size or color may be changed. These questions are more confusing as it is important to pay attention to more subtle differences between the possible answers.

In the following example the answer is 7.
Examinees may wrongly choose answers 2 or 6.

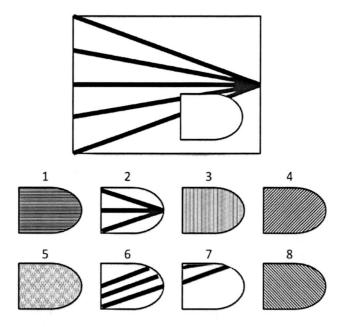

In the below example, note the directions and pay attention to what appears on the front and what is in the background. Answers 2, 3 and 7 are intended to create a short diversion and contribute to the examinee's confusion and stress. After taking a closer look and identifying the differences between the different options it becomes clear that answers 1 and 6 are the only candidates. These two answers are very similar and the only difference is the foreground / background order. In answer 1 the black curve is in the foreground, as in the big picture, so that's correct.

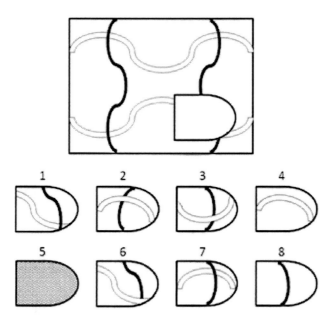

A few comments regarding the Raven's Matrices tests:

- Matrices tests are widely used, however usually the level of difficulty is not high.
- The official Raven's Matrixes test contains 60 questions, all included in the example tests section below. Some of these questions are difficult, some are very difficult, but the children IQ tests are not that difficult. Nevertheless we decided to include them in this book for three main reasons:
  - Knowing the 60 questions will help to answer similar questions in case they do appear.
  - It's great practice for all types of spatial perception and pattern recognition questions.
  - Most children love these questions.

  Therefore our recommendation is to let the child experience some of these questions without pressure and with emphasis on the fact that these questions are more difficult than the expected test.
- The five example tests are arranged in order of increasing difficulty. If the child finds one test difficult, do not let them continue to the next, more difficult tests. Let them redo the tests that were already done.

Sample Tests

On the following pages you will find dozens of sample tests of different types. The number of sample tests of each type was determined according to two main criteria:

- The importance of the practice for the particular type of test. Areas for which practice may significantly improve the score will contain more sample tests. For other types of tests fewer samples are provided, just to allow the child to understand the principles and reduce the pressure during the actual test.
- The probability that a certain type of test will appear in a children's IQ test, based on recent years' experience.

At the beginning of each section you will find a short explanation, similar to the expiation that usually appears in actual tests. If the child is young and cannot yet read, the explanation should be read and possibly interpreted to the child.

The allocated time for each test, according to the child age, is specified as well. The time will most likely not be sufficient for answering all questions. The tests are built this way so more gifted children will be able to achieve a higher score by answering more answers. As recommended before, the best practice is to randomly guess the remaining answers when time is over, however in the sample tests you should let your child complete the tests after the given time in order to practice some more.

As this section's audience age may vary from 6-year-old pre-school children to 13-year-old children getting ready for junior-high, it includes tests in different levels. When relevant, the sample tests in each section are ordered from the easiest to the most challenging. Each child should start from the first test and move forward as long as they can cope with the difficulty level. There is no point in pushing your child to struggle with problems above the expected level for a specific age. This may lead to counterproductive frustration and antagonism. Encourage your child to do the best they can. When you feel that the level is too high, just stop. If the child is cooperating, you can try solving some of the remaining questions together, exposing the child to more strategies and mature problem-solving methodologies.

General Knowledge Sample Tests

 Instruction:
Following you will find ten questions covering different fields of knowledge. Four possible answers are suggested for each question. You must choose one answer, the one that best answers the question.

 Available time by age:

Age	6	7	8	9	10	11	12	13
Time (Minutes)	15	12	10	8	8	8	6	6

General Knowledge Sample Test 1

1. Who judges points in a soccer match?
   a. a judge
   b. a referee
   c. a proctor
   d. an inspector

2. Which word means fortunate?
   a. genial
   b. lucky
   c. lively
   d. rich

3. Which word means behave badly?
   a. act up
   b. act out
   c. act on
   d. react

4. Which word completes the expression: "dead as a _____ nail".
   a. finger
   b. steel
   c. toe
   d. door

5. When you put in for a job, you are _____ .
   a. an applicant
   b. a customer
   c. a claimant
   d. an expert

6. When a person says: "I took it with a pinch of salt", he means:
   a. he ate it with some salt.
   b. he sprinkled the food with salt.
   c. he felt some doubt whether it was altogether true.
   d. he ate something he doesn't really like.

7. What is the person who pays rent called?
   a. an occupant
   b. a tenant
   c. a landlord
   d. a housekeeper

8. Which word does not mean lazy?
   a. idle
   b. inactive
   c. industrious
   d. sluggish

9. What do people sing at Christmas?
   a. carols
   b. lullabies
   c. lyrics
   d. gospel

10. Which word does not mean lovely?
   a. pleasant
   b. amusing
   c. gorgeous
   d. faithful

General Knowledge Sample Test 2

1. Who offers a house or an apartment for rent?
   a. a landlady
   b. a charwoman
   c. a tenant
   d. a housekeeper

2. What do you put on the finger to protect it while sewing?
   a. a thumb
   b. a thimble
   c. a thorn
   d. a glove

3. Who sees that the rules are obeyed in a baseball game?
   a. a judge
   b. a referee
   c. an eye witness
   d. an umpire

4. What word does not refer to babies?
   a. pacifier
   b. milkweed
   c. cradle
   d. diaper

5. Which word completes the proverb: "Every _____ has its day."
   a. tiger
   b. dog
   c. horse
   d. night

6. Which word does not mean dismal?
   a. queasy
   b. lugubrious
   c. gloomy
   d. grim

7. "A bit" means ___.
   a. some thing to eat
   b. to help someone
   c. a large chunk
   d. a small amount

8. "About time" means ___.
    a. at the right time
    b. soon
    c. at last
    d. more or less

9. "Across the board" means ___.
    a. everyone or everything is included
    b. to travel between countries
    c. uninteresting
    d. jump sea

10. To "act up" means ___.
    a. to share an idea
    b. to behave badly
    c. to pretend to be rich
    d. to climb

General Knowledge Sample Test 3

1. A man "after my own heart" means ___.
    a. liking the same things as me
    b. looks like me
    c. follows me
    d. a man in love

2. "Against the clock" means ___.
    a. a new record
    b. a test of speed or time
    c. an impossible task
    d. at the last moment

3. "All along" means ___.
    a. all the time
    b. to agree
    c. altogether
    d. for the whole length

4. "All hours" means ___.
    a. at regular times
    b. at irregular times
    c. every hour
    d. around the clock

5. "Along in years" means ___.
    a. getting old
    b. getting tired
    c. becoming successful
    d. ancient

6. "And then some" means ___.
    a. not many
    b. and only a few
    c. wait before
    d. and a lot more

7. If you are "in the family way", you are ___.
    a. shy
    b. popular
    c. pregnant
    d. getting married

8. If it's "in the wind", it's ___.
   a. imminent
   b. lost
   c. furnished
   d. something to think about

9. If you are "in the dog house", you are ___.
   a. enthusiastic
   b. in trouble
   c. happy
   d. friendly

10. "In the pink" means to be ___.
   a. drunk
   b. healthy
   c. rich
   d. ready

General Knowledge Sample Test 4

1. To "iron out" means to ___ .
    a. complete small details
    b. make problems
    c. plan ahead
    d. bypass an issue

2. "In toto" means ___ .
    a. no where
    b. something
    c. everything
    d. a small chance

3. The "ins and outs" are ___ .
    a. the small details
    b. everyone
    c. complications
    d. the main point

4. If something is "in your hair", it's ___ .
    a. interesting
    b. amusing
    c. scary
    d. annoying

5. "In hand" means ___ .
    a. unmanageable
    b. under control
    c. difficult
    d. available

6. "In the nick of time" means ___ .
    a. too late
    b. on time
    c. in time
    d. very quickly

7. To "raise eyebrows" is to ___ .
    a. question something
    b. be afraid
    c. shock
    d. faking

8. If something will happen "rain or shine", it'll happen ___.
    a. at some point, but we don't know when
    b. outside
    c. suddenly
    d. no matter what

9. To "rattle off" is to ___.
    a. break something
    b. say things quickly
    c. be old
    d. throw something

10. "Razzle dazzle" is ___.
    a. a fancy display
    b. an unusual event
    c. something impossible
    d. a jigsaw puzzle

General Knowledge Sample Test 5

1. The "rear end" is ___ .
   a. the start of something
   b. a one way street
   c. the back part
   d. outermost part

2. To "ride out" something is ___ .
   a. finish successfully
   b. to survive safely
   c. give up
   d. to train a hourse

3. If it's to the "right and left" it's ___ .
   a. rare
   b. very quick
   c. all around
   d. the wrong way

4. If something "rings a bell", it ___ .
   a. makes a lot of noise
   b. is frightening
   c. want to get in
   d. sounds familiar

5. To "rip into" means to ___ .
   a. enjoy
   b. attack
   c. savour
   d. denounce

6. To "run away with" means to ___ .
   a. lend
   b. steal
   c. borrow
   d. overcome

7. If you are a boy what gender are you?
   a. female
   b. guy
   c. boy
   d. male

8. What is the meaning of wind?
    a. wind is cold air
    b. wind is cool air
    c. wind is air in motion
    d. wind is warm air

9. What is the term for the study of flags?
    a. A.   Culturology
    b. B.   Heraldology
    c. C.   Vexillology
    d. D.   Patriology

10. If you are interested in helping people, and you value having a variety of things to do, then you may choose a career as a _____
    a. farmer
    b. sports agent
    c. guidance counselor
    d. lab scientist

General Knowledge Sample Test 6

1. What is the heaviest naturally occurring metal on Earth?
   a. Plutonium
   b. Uranium
   c. Gold
   d. Platinum

2. 2. How many legs do butterflies have?
   a. 8
   b. 6
   c. 4
   d. 2

3. What is the most populous country in the world?
   a. Bangladesh
   b. China
   c. India
   d. USA

4. Which state is the biggest in the US?
   a. Alaska
   b. Florida
   c. Texas
   d. Washington

5. Which is the largest country (by area) in the world?
   a. India
   b. Canada
   c. China
   d. Russia

6. What is the common name for Aurora Borealis?
   a. Northern Lights
   b. Southern Lights
   c. Princess A
   d. Princess Australia

7. What is the most common non-contagious disease in the world?
   a. common cold
   b. cancer
   c. tooth decay
   d. arteriosclerosis

8. What was the last recorded album of Beatles?
    a. Abbey road
    b. Let it be
    c. Rolling stone
    d. Yellow submarine

9. What instrument did Miles Davis, the jazz musician, play?
    a. piano
    b. clarinet
    c. trumpet
    d. bass

10. In which sport could you get into a headlock?
    a. kung fu
    b. wrestling
    c. boxing
    d. judo

General Knowledge Sample Test 7

1. In which country was golf first played?
   a. Scotland
   b. America
   c. England
   d. Japan

2. Which is the sport where you could be out 'leg before wicket', or 'hit a six'?
   a. Golf
   b. Polo
   c. Hockey
   d. Cricket

3. 13. When was baseball first played in the US?
   a. 1901
   b. 1846
   c. 1245
   d. 2005

4. 14. In which sport would you use a 'sand iron'?
   a. golf
   b. pool
   c. tennis
   d. table tennis

5. What is the largest mammal in the world?
   a. giraffe
   b. blue whale
   c. Asian elefent
   d. African elephant

6. Where did reggae music originate?
   a. USA
   b. Germany
   c. Jamaica
   d. Rajasthan

7. Who was the creator of Jeeves and Wooster?
   a. P.G. Wodehouse
   b. Oscar Wilde
   c. Dr. Seuss
   d. Mark Twain

8. Who painted the ceiling of the Sistine Chapel?
    a. Leonardo Da Vinci
    b. Michelangelo
    c. Raphael
    d. Botticelli

9. Who was the writer of Alice's Adventures in Wonderland?
    a. Rudyard Kipling
    b. Mark Twain
    c. Oscar Wilde
    d. Lewis Carroll

10. After which famous person was the teddy bear named?
    a. Theodore the bear
    b. Teddy Pendergrass
    c. Theodore Roosevelt
    d. Theo Huxtable

General Knowledge Sample Test 8

1. Which is the smallest ocean in the world?
    a. Pacific Ocean
    b. Arctic Ocean
    c. Atlantic Ocean
    d. Indian Ocean

2. What is the rhino's horn made of?
    a. Bone
    b. Hair
    c. Stone
    d. Ivory

3. Who created Snoopy?
    a. Hergé
    b. Charles M. Schulz
    c. Dr. Seuss
    d. Louis Carole

4. Who was the first non-royal to appear on a UK postage stamp?
    a. William Shakespeare
    b. Issac Newton
    c. Christopher Columbus
    d. Galileo Galilei

5. What is the capital city of Afghanistan?
    a. Kandahar
    b. Kabul
    c. Afghanistan City
    d. Katmandu

6. What is the capital city of Israel?
    a. Tel-Aviv
    b. Palestine
    c. Jerusalem
    d. Tiberius

7. What is the capital city of France?
    a. Paris
    b. Zurich
    c. London
    d. San-Michele

8. What is the capital city of Russia?
   a. Moscow
   b. Leningrad
   c. San Petersburg
   d. Siberia

9. What is the capital city of Japan?
   a. Beijing
   b. Osaka
   c. Tokyo
   d. Seoul

10. How many Arab nations are there
   a. a few
   b. less than 10
   c. between 10 to 20
   d. more than 20

General Knowledge Sample Test 9

1. Where is the White House located?
   - A. Washington D.C.
   - B. Pennsylvania
   - C. New York
   - D. New Jersey

2. What number are you supposed to call in case of an emergency?
   - A. 912
   - B. 919
   - C. 911
   - D. 324

3. Which animal is the fastest in the world?
   - A. cheetah
   - B. lion
   - C. gazelle
   - D. ostrich

4. What are the three colors in the American Flag?
   - A. red, white, and blue
   - B. black, pink, and purple
   - C. red, pink, and green
   - D. black, white, and orange

5. What is the purpose of July 4?
   - A. Just a celebration
   - B. to celebrate the troops
   - C. Christian holiday
   - D. US Independence Day

6. What is the two longest rivers in the world?
   - A. The Nile and the Amazonas
   - B. The Red river
   - C. Mississippi river
   - D. Comite river

7. Abraham Lincoln was which president?
   - A. 16st
   - B. 17th
   - C. 1st
   - D. 19th

8. What of the following is the most popular sport in the United States?
   A.   Baseball
   B.   Volleyball
   C.   Tennis
   D.   basketball

9. On which planet are we living?
   A.   Venus
   B.   Earth
   C.   Pluto
   D.   Jupiter

10. What state is the biggest in the U.S.?
   A.   Louisiana
   B.   Pennsylvania
   C.   Hawaii
   D.   Alaska

General Knowledge Sample Test 10

1. Which metal is heavier?
   A. Silver
   B. Tin
   C. Diamond
   D. Gold

2. How many legs do butterflies have?
   A. 12
   B. 8
   C. 6
   D. 4

3. What is the largest mammal in the world?
   A. Elephant
   B. Cheetah
   C. Blue Whale
   D. Pelican

4. What is the rhino's horn made of?
   A. silk
   B. bone
   C. glass
   D. hair

5. Which is the smallest ocean in the world?
   A. Atlantic Ocean
   B. Arctic Ocean
   C. English Ocean
   D. Tiger Ocean

6. How many letters are there in the English alphabet?
   A. 26
   B. 24
   C. 22
   D. 20

7. How many stars are present in the national flag of the United States of America?
   A. 52
   B. 50
   C. 40
   D. 45

8. Which astronaut placed the first flag on the moon?
   A.   Buzz Aldrin
   B.   Neil Armstrong
   C.   Rakesh Sharma
   D.   Ed White

9. Which is the capital of India?
   A.   New Delhi
   B.   Mumbai
   C.   Kolkota
   D.   Kabul

10. What is the largest planet?
   A.   Pluto
   B.   Earth
   C.   Uranus
   D.   Jupiter

General Knowledge Sample Test 11

1. The INNER PART of the Earth is called.....
    A.   INNER CORE
    B.   OUTER CORE
    C.   INNER MANTLE
    D.   CRUST

2. What is the number of plants in the solar system?
    A.   eight planets, and five dwarf planets
    B.   eight planets, and one dwarf planets
    C.   five planets, and five dwarf planets
    D.   five planets, and four dwarf planets

3. What is the coldest continent of Earth?
    A.   Asia
    B.   America
    C.   Europe
    D.   Antarctica

4. What is a food chain?
    A.   saving the environment
    B.   humans eating animals
    C.   Famous chain of restaurants
    D.   the eating relationships between species within and ecosystem

5. What type of food is bread?
    A.   grain
    B.   dairy
    C.   fruit
    D.   vegetables

6. What type of food is milk?
    A.   dairy
    B.   vegetables
    C.   fruit
    D.   grain

7. Which of the following is a junk food?
    A.   grapes
    B.   pizza
    C.   juice
    D.   milk

8. Who was the first president of the United States?
   A.   George W. Bush
   B.   George Washington
   C.   Abraham Lincoln
   D.   Henry Ford

9. What is the tallest animal living on land?
   A.   Giraffe
   B.   Elephant
   C.   Bear
   D.   Kangaroo

10. How many moons does Jupiter have?
    A.   Jupiter has no moons
    B.   1 moon
    C.   2 moons
    D.   more than 60 moons

General Knowledge Sample Test 12

1. A cow had how many stomachs?
   A.   1
   B.   2
   C.   4
   D.   5

2. Which is the language spoken by most people?
   A.   Arabic
   B.   English
   C.   Spanish
   D.   Mandarin

3. Who painted the Mona Lisa?
   A.   Sandro Botticelli
   B.   Michelangelo
   C.   Leonardo Da Vinci
   D.   Raphael

4. Who was Abraham Lincoln to America?
   A.   foreigm minister
   B.   founder
   C.   vice president
   D.   president

5. Snow White ate this fruit that had poison in it.
   A.   orange
   B.   mango
   C.   apple
   D.   pineapple

6. How long does it take for the Earth to go around the sun?
   A.   30 days
   B.   24 hours
   C.   1 year
   D.   360 days

7. How did the Titanic sink?
   A.   too many people
   B.   hit an iceberg
   C.   the luggage was too heavy
   D.   the water was all frozen

8. How many months are in a year?
   A.   7
   B.   30
   C.   365
   D.   12

9. Who was the most famous escape artist of the 20th century?
   A.   Harry Houdini
   B.   Amanda Bynes
   C.   Layla Pete
   D.   Karin Ayne

10. Who is known as the mother of the black civil rights movement?
    A.   Margaret Thatcher
    B.   Michelle Obama
    C.   Rosa Parks
    D.   Kiran Bedi

Synonyms Sample Tests

 Instruction:
Following you will find 10 questions. Each question contains a word and four possible answers. You must choose one of the answers, the word that has the same (or nearly the same) meaning (the synonym).

 Available time by age:

Age	6	7	8	9	10	11	12	13
Time (Minutes)	12	10	10	8	8	6	6	5

Synonyms Sample Test 1

1. ANGRY
   A. happy
   B. mad
   C. tired
   D. sad

2. AMAZING
   A. small
   B. irregular
   C. crazy
   D. incredible

3. FAIR
   A. equal
   B. large
   C. loose
   D. unbalance

4. HUGE
   A. light
   B. determined
   C. tiny
   D. giant

5. HILARIOUS
   A. very smart
   B. very funny
   C. very small
   D. very large

6. LOVELY
   A. very shy
   B. very expensive
   C. very nice
   D. very tired

7. ATTACK
   A. protect
   B. resist
   C. stop
   D. defend

8. TWIST
   A. open
   B. tighten
   C. lock
   D. turn

9. MAKE
   A. do
   B. destroy
   C. build
   D. clean

10. SEE
    A. decide
    B. hear
    C. do
    D. understand

Synonyms Sample Test 2

1. MIX
    A. cook
    B. bake
    C. stir
    D. burn

2. RATTLE
    A. entertain
    B. vibrate
    C. maintain
    D. move

3. HANDBAG
    A. shoe
    B. hat
    C. belt
    D. purse

4. ROBBER
    A. officer
    B. police
    C. thief
    D. banker

5. HELP
    A. assistant
    B. aid
    C. payment
    D. application

6. FEAR
    A. cry
    B. hide
    C. run
    D. terror

7. HOTEL
    A. bed
    B. stay
    C. inn
    D. room

8. DOOR
    A. key
    B. gate
    C. wall
    D. tunnel

9. ECSTATIC
    A. very happy
    B. very sad
    C. very loud
    D. very small

10. WILD
    A. crazy
    B. casual
    C. calm
    D. reserved

Synonyms Sample Test 3

1. VIGILANT
   A. passionate
   B. powerful
   C. remote
   D. aware

2. IMMATURE
   A. retired
   B. experienced
   C. old
   D. juvenile

3. WHOLESOME
   A. evil
   B. bad
   C. healthy
   D. painful

4. FRIENDLY
   A. amiable
   B. hopeful
   C. good
   D. mean

5. GRATEFUL
   A. supportive
   B. thankful
   C. healthy
   D. kind

6. LOCAL
   A. distant
   B. global
   C. nearby
   D. regional

7. CLEAR
   A. clean
   B. cloudy
   C. transparent
   D. polluted

8. MILD
   A. various
   B. weak
   C. moderate
   D. strong

9. KEEN
   A. articulate
   B. easy
   C. loose
   D. sharp

10. OFFENSIVE
    A. cruel
    B. unpleasant
    C. normal
    D. aware

Synonyms Sample Test 4

1. MAYBE
   A. doubtfully
   B. surely
   C. perhaps
   D. possibly

2. SOMETIMES
   A. rarely
   B. only
   C. occasionally
   D. often

3. OFTEN
   A. seldom
   B. occasionally
   C. never
   D. frequently

4. CERTAINLY
   A. maybe
   B. surely
   C. possibly
   D. probably

5. TRULY
   A. really
   B. rapidly
   C. carefully
   D. passionately

6. ALWAYS
   A. never
   B. constantly
   C. occasionally
   D. seldom

7. WARNING
   A. attention
   B. emergency
   C. victim
   D. danger

8. AMAZEMENT
   A. expectation
   B. assumption
   C. astonishment
   D. passion

9. TEACHER
   A. discussion
   B. president
   C. leader
   D. instructor

10. RESPECT
    A. destruction
    B. degradation
    C. humiliation
    D. honor

Synonyms Sample Test 5

1. PERIL
    A. doom
    B. happiness
    C. action
    D. danger

2. MEETING
    A. greeting
    B. encounter
    C. sale
    D. announcement

3. AFFECTION
    A. hate
    B. danger
    C. dislike
    D. love

4. LEAGUE
    A. collective
    B. alliance
    C. individual
    D. group

5. ODOR
    A. smell
    B. sound
    C. taste
    D. sight

6. CHOICE
    A. stake
    B. decision
    C. idea
    D. position

7. LIBERTY
    A. law
    B. right
    C. moral
    D. freedom

8. REGION
    A. island
    B. nation
    C. country
    D. territory

9. DECLINE
    A. mountain
    B. discipline
    C. hill
    D. descent

10. CHOIR
    A. chorus
    B. council
    C. team
    D. group

Synonyms Sample Test 6

1. OUTCAST
   A. specialist
   B. nomad
   C. exile
   D. expert

2. RECOMMENDATION
   A. rejection
   B. idea
   C. claim
   D. advice

3. BEVERAGE
   A. liquid
   B. potion
   C. food
   D. drink

4. HUMANITY
   A. woman
   B. land
   C. country
   D. mankind

5. DIPLOMAT
   A. revolt
   B. combatant
   C. refugee
   D. ambassador

6. MISTAKE
   A. omission
   B. sentence
   C. error
   D. paragraph

7. CONSERVATION
   A. environment
   B. preservation
   C. agriculture
   D. technology

8. ENTHUSIASM
   A. passion
   B. goal
   C. will
   D. entertainment

9. CONSCIOUSNESS
   A. vision
   B. understanding
   C. books
   D. awareness

10. RESULT
    A. decision
    B. cause
    C. outcome
    D. data

Synonyms Sample Test 7

1. UNIQUE
   A. auspicious
   B. numerous
   C. distinguished
   D. singular

2. RESTIVE
   A. pacific
   B. restless
   C. calm
   D. festive

3. GRIEVOUS
   A. superfluous
   B. shameful
   C. regretful
   D. minor

4. MOTTLED
   A. divided
   B. regional
   C. homogenous
   D. dappled

5. AMBULATORY
   A. quiescent
   B. stationary
   C. peripatetic
   D. permanent

6. DISINTERESTED
   A. partisan
   B. inclined
   C. uninterested
   D. impartial

7. NEFARIOUS
   A. foreshadowing
   B. nebulous
   C. villainous
   D. blessed

8. PURE
   A. corrupt
   B. lucid
   C. unadulterated
   D. opaque

9. NEOPHYTE
   A. parsimony
   B. guru
   C. expert
   D. fledgling

10. PAUCITY
    A. perfection
    B. dearth
    C. deterrent
    D. damage

Synonyms Sample Test 8
(A slightly different version of this type of test)

 Instruction:
Following you will find 10 questions. Each question contains a sentence and four possible answers. You must choose one of the answers, the one that best interprets the underlined words in the sentence.

 Available time by age:

Age	6	7	8	9	10	11	12	13
Time (Minutes)	12	10	10	8	8	6	6	5

1. Chris told us <u>to hand in</u> our term paper next Monday.
   a. to write our paper by hand
   b. to submit
   c. to correct
   d. to proof-read

2. Professor Wilson is a wonderful teacher but there are <u>too many assignments</u> in his course.
   a. His marks are always low.
   b. There are too many books to read.
   c. He often gives homework.
   d. There are too many students in his course.

3. Since I wanted to buy the new book, I had to <u>put in an order</u> through the store manager.
   a. The store-manager didn't want to buy it.
   b. The book was out of print.
   c. I had to ask for it to be bought for me.
   d. The computer was out of order.

4. Did you know <u>it's down to three of us</u> for the job in the library?
   a. The three of us will be working in the library.
   b. There are only three applicants left.
   c. The library only hires three students.
   d. At least three students will be retained.

5. I'll really have to <u>hit the books</u> this weekend.
     a. I have to tidy my room.
     b. There is a book fair this weekend.
     c. My books need a cover.
     d. I have to study.

6. <u>To major in</u> astrophysics you need an extra math course.
     a. To get higher grades in astrophysics
     b. To specialize in astrophysics
     c. To finish your astrophysics paper
     d. To better understand the astrophysics course

7. Did you know Mark is a <u>sophomore</u>?
     a. Mark is a second-year student.
     b. Mark majors in philosophy.
     c. Mark has a special grant.
     d. Mark's parents are both university professors.

8. I haven't <u>completed all the prerequisites</u> for this course.
     a. I still have to fill in some papers.
     b. I have to finish some assignments.
     c. I haven't done enough research.
     d. I have to do some other courses first.

9. This year I will need to find <u>off-campus housing</u>.
     a. I will live on the campus.
     b. I will buy a house next to the campus.
     c. I will live outside the campus.
     d. The campus will provide a house for me.

10. Alice, if I were you, I'd <u>skip the meeting</u>.
     a. Alice should prepare for the meeting.
     b. Alice should put the meeting on her agenda.
     c. The meeting is going to be cancelled.
     d. Alice shouldn't bother to go to the meeting.

Antonyms Sample Tests

 Instruction:
Following you will find 10 questions. Each question contains a word in capital letters and four possible answers. You must choose one of the answers: the word that is most nearly opposite in meaning to the word in capital letters (the best antonyms).

 Available time by age:

Age	6	7	8	9	10	11	12	13
Time (Minutes)	12	10	10	8	8	6	6	5

Words Antonyms Sample Test 1

1. ADVANTAGE
    A. blessing
    B. fortune
    C. problem
    D. illness

2. MISERY
    A. trouble
    B. pleasure
    C. suffering
    D. luck

3. SOLUTION
    A. doubt
    B. result
    C. theory
    D. dilemma

4. MOIST
    A. humid
    B. cold
    C. dry
    D. gassy

5. STEER
    A. drive
    B. follow
    C. extend
    D. cease

6. RESIDENT
    A. visitor
    B. owner
    C. company
    D. citizen

7. MAGNIFICENT
    A. ugly
    B. gorgeous
    C. normal
    D. thrilling

8. DIFFERENT
    A. other
    B. unchanged
    C. opposite
    D. identical

9. DOWNSTAIRS
    A. below
    B. above
    C. beside
    D. atop

10. OBSERVE
    A. inspect
    B. deny
    C. glance
    D. witness

Words Antonyms Sample Test 2

1. BRIEF
   A. long
   B. stable
   C. strong
   D. short

2. BLINDNESS
   A. handicap
   B. vision
   C. scent
   D. alertness

3. UNLIKE
   A. different
   B. reverse
   C. similar
   D. separate

4. FAN
   A. performer
   B. friend
   C. follower
   D. critic

5. AMBITIOUS
   A. hopeful
   B. lazy
   C. aimless
   D. spirited

6. ORIGIN
   A. reason
   B. detour
   C. understanding
   D. destination

7. CERTAIN
   A. convinced
   B. unsure
   C. calm
   D. false

8. DARK
   A. shady
   B. dim
   C. brilliant
   D. colorful

9. METHODICAL
   A. random
   B. orderly
   C. organized
   D. crazy

10. OPPONENT
    A. observer
    B. enemy
    C. ally
    D. rival

Words Antonyms Sample Test 3

1. CLING
   A. detach
   B. clutch
   C. hug
   D. slice

2. CONTAIN
   A. exclude
   B. accept
   C. unite
   D. remove

3. PREVENT
   A. avoid
   B. interrupt
   C. stop
   D. cause

4. COMMON
   A. standard
   B. unusual
   C. scary
   D. super

5. SCHEDULED
   A. assigned
   B. prepared
   C. unplanned
   D. late

6. ARCTIC
   A. chilly
   B. tropical
   C. frozen
   D. melted

7. PREDATOR
   A. prey
   B. buyer
   C. hunter
   D. farmer

8. CLEVER
   A. splendid
   B. smart
   C. sassy
   D. stupid

9. CONSIDER
   A. think
   B. ignore
   C. finish
   D. study

10. ATTRACT
   A. depend
   B. delight
   C. disgust
   D. disable

Words Antonyms Sample Test 4

1. LAST
   A. early
   B. closing
   C. ending
   D. primary

2. DISTRESS
   A. headache
   B. pleasure
   C. luck
   D. suffering

3. CAPTIVITY
   A. slavery
   B. permission
   C. freedom
   D. limitation

4. CRAFTY
   A. honest
   B. bright
   C. deceitful
   D. scientific

5. RESIST
   A. adjust
   B. remain
   C. decline
   D. yield

6. REVEAL
   A. develop
   B. showcase
   C. cover
   D. thwart

7. SURVIVE
   A. recover
   B. expire
   C. withstand
   D. flee

8. DETEST
   A. adore
   B. withhold
   C. injure
   D. assist

9. CAREFREE
   A. easygoing
   B. worried
   C. relaxed
   D. cautious

10. BICKER
   A. debate
   B. surrender
   C. concur
   D. hassle

Words Antonyms Sample Test 5

1. DEBATE
   A. agree
   B. tame
   C. dispute
   D. ignore

2. HAVOC
   A. wonder
   B. peace
   C. chaos
   D. warfare

3. EXCAVATE
   A. scrape
   B. hollow
   C. bury
   D. mask

4. ABSURD
   A. batty
   B. sensible
   C. certain
   D. insane

5. PEDESTRIAN
   A. motorist
   B. hiker
   C. galloper
   D. sailor

6. SOLITARY
   A. friendly
   B. lonely
   C. isolated
   D. together

7. SOAR
   A. elevate
   B. float
   C. mount
   D. land

8. ATHLETIC
   A. frail
   B. muscular
   C. energetic
   D. intelligent

9. CRITICIZE
   A. punish
   B. praise
   C. blame
   D. approve

10. ACCOMPLISH
    A. exhaust
    B. manage
    C. blunder
    D. cease

Words Antonyms Sample Test 6

1. NOVICE
   A. beginner
   B. expert
   C. amateur
   D. competitor

2. MAXIMUM
   A. sufficient
   B. largest
   C. merest
   D. limited

3. DETERIORATE
   A. corrode
   B. upgrade
   C. decorate
   D. debilitate

4. DRASTIC
   A. lax
   B. loving
   C. brutal
   D. strict

5. CONSERVE
   A. support
   B. stash
   C. sustain
   D. squander

6. MINUTE
   A. mighty
   B. puny
   C. fine
   D. immense

7. DOMINATE
   A. oversee
   B. debate
   C. rile
   D. submit

8. EFFICIENT
   A. unproductive
   B. slipshod
   C. systematic
   D. proficient

9. TERMINATE
   A. cancel
   B. lapse
   C. restrict
   D. initiate

10. GENERATE
    A. sever
    B. develop
    C. demolish
    D. multiply

Words Antonyms Sample Test 7

1. COUNTERFEIT
   A. unmarked
   B. assumed
   C. fraudulent
   D. genuine

2. ABRUPT
   A. hurried
   B. impulsive
   C. methodical
   D. gradual

3. BYSTANDER
   A. participant
   B. detective
   C. colleague
   D. pedestrian

4. INFAMOUS
   A. sincere
   B. glorious
   C. notorious
   D. outrageous

5. GRIM
   A. meek
   B. grave
   C. lighthearted
   D. hopeful

6. FRUITLESS
   A. useless
   B. futile
   C. purposeful
   D. profitable

7. MURKY
   A. luminous
   B. charitable
   C. smoky
   D. miserable

8. UTMOST
   A. remotest
   B. minimal
   C. supreme
   D. limitless

9. COW
   A. condense
   B. chill
   C. comfort
   D. startle

10. LAVISH
   A. unsightly
   B. petite
   C. awful
   D. economical

Words Antonyms Sample Test 8

1. AGONY
    A. comfort
    B. anguish
    C. success
    D. grief

2. MYRIAD
    A. mass
    B. scarcity
    C. void
    D. excess

3. GRATIFY
    A. puncture
    B. coddle
    C. disappoint
    D. fatigue

4. CULTIVATE
    A. labor
    B. neglect
    C. renounce
    D. further

5. MULTIPLY
    A. bisect
    B. accumulate
    C. lessen
    D. deliver

6. MISUNDERSTAND
    A. grasp
    B. analyze
    C. nurture
    D. instruct

7. SUBSEQUENT
    A. consequential
    B. illogical
    C. later
    D. former

8. MANUAL
    A. improved
    B. antiquated
    C. standard
    D. automated

9. JUSTIFY
    A. explain
    B. rationalize
    C. apologize
    D. invalidate

10. PUNISHMENT
    A. profit
    B. purgatory
    C. penalty
    D. bounty

Odd One Out Sample Tests

 Instruction:
Following you will find 10 questions. Each question contains four words or terms. You should choose the one that is different, the one that does not belong to the group the other three belong to.

 Available time by age:

Age	6	7	8	9	10	11	12	13
Time (Minutes)	12	10	10	8	8	6	6	5

Odd One Out Sample Test 1

1.
   A. table
   B. chair
   C. cupboard
   D. wood

2.
   A. chest
   B. ear
   C. lip
   D. nose

3.
   A. silver
   B. gold
   C. platinum
   D. ivory

4.
   A. jacket
   B. shirt
   C. trousers
   D. cloth

5.
   A. carbon
   B. copper
   C. iron
   D. aluminum

6.
   A. walk
   B. run
   C. sit
   D. jog

7.
   A. paper
   B. pen
   C. pencil
   D. crayon

8.
   A. bungalow
   B. cottage
   C. farm
   D. hut

9.
   A. milk
   B. cheese
   C. butter
   D. yoghurt

10.
   A. brook
   B. stream
   C. river
   D. pond

Odd One Out Sample Test 2

1.
   A. pool
   B. water
   C. lake
   D. pond

2.
   A. arrow
   B. dagger
   C. spear
   D. shield

3.
   A. eagle
   B. cloud
   C. squirrel
   D. airplane

4.
   A. table
   B. chair
   C. sofa
   D. stool

5.
   A. dog
   B. cow
   C. lion
   D. horse

6.
   A. Earth
   B. Pluto
   C. Mars
   D. Moon

7.
   A. August
   B. December
   C. November
   D. January

8.
   A. flute
   B. bugle
   C. guitar
   D. trumpet

9.
   A. 232
   B. 450
   C. 301
   D. 122

10.
   A. guitar
   B. violin
   C. harp
   D. trumpet

Odd One Out Sample Test 3

1.
   A. israel
   B. greestan
   C. england
   D. egypt

2.
   A. apple
   B. orange
   C. ear
   D. lemon

3.
   A. rain
   B. father
   C. mother
   D. sister

4.
   A. dog
   B. cat
   C. yo-yo
   D. cow

5.
   A. water
   B. milk
   C. tea
   D. banana

6.
   A. many
   B. two
   C. five
   D. eight

7.
   A. teacher
   B. lesson
   C. ox
   D. class

8.
   A. rainbow
   B. yellow
   C. red
   D. white

9.
   A. summer
   B. winter
   C. spring
   D. sun

10.
   A. ball
   B. doll
   C. friend
   D. yo-yo

Odd One Out Sample Test 4

1.
   A. face
   B. hand
   C. ear
   D. tattoo

2.
   A. skirt
   B. socks
   C. rug
   D. dress

3.
   A. Mother
   B. Brother
   C. Friend
   D. Daughter

4.
   A. Shoe
   B. Sandal
   C. Glove
   D. Boot

5.
   A. Lake
   B. Forest
   C. Ocean
   D. River

6.
   A. Seat
   B. Wheel
   C. Door
   D. Oven

7.
   A. Car
   B. Seat
   C. Train
   D. Motorcycle

8.
   A. Happy
   B. Grumpy
   C. Joy
   D. Excited

9.
   A. Rice
   B. Pork
   C. Chicken
   D. Beef

10.
   A. Eye
   B. Radar
   C. Level
   D. Star

Odd One Out Sample Test 5

1.
   A. coat
   B. scarf
   C. gloves
   D. shorts

2.
   A. trousers
   B. shirt
   C. shorts
   D. jeans

3.
   A. pen
   B. paper
   C. chair
   D. rubber

4.
   A. window
   B. table
   C. wall
   D. floor

5.
   A. paper
   B. chair
   C. desk
   D. table

6.
   A. kangaroo
   B. bedbug
   C. chicken
   D. frog

7.
   A. bedroom
   B. classroom
   C. kitchen
   D. living room

8.
   E. boy
   F. female
   G. woman
   H. girl

9.
   A. Cabbage
   B. Pineapple
   C. Apple
   D. Orange

10.
   A. Doctor
   B. Vet
   C. Norse
   D. Chiropractor

Missing Words Sample Tests

Instruction:
Following you will find ten sentences. Each sentence is missing a word. After each sentence you will find four possible words or terms for completing the sentence. Choose the one that completes the sentence in the best way.

Available time by age:

Age	6	7	8	9	10	11	12	13
Time (Minutes)	15	12	10	8	8	8	6	6

Missing Words Sample Test 1

1. Sometimes the _____ has a face.
   - A. comes
   - B. bright
   - C. full
   - D. moon

2. A circle is _____ like an orange.
   - A. fresh
   - B. round
   - C. eaten
   - D. cream

3. Mom told us to _____ our toys.
   - A. pencil
   - B. food
   - C. take
   - D. tree

4. _____ need water just like dogs.
   - A. Cats
   - B. Done
   - C. Food
   - D. Drinks

5. Sparrows were building a _____.
   - A. fell
   - B. nest
   - C. guess
   - D. smile

6. Children were _____ at the clown.
     A. moon
     B. tomorrow
     C. potato
     D. laughing

7. The kite fell from the _____.
     A. apple
     B. hope
     C. sky
     D. seven

8. If you try, you can _____ any problem.
     A. flour
     B. quack
     C. solve
     D. seem

9. They always got up _____ to go to school.
     A. early
     B. bike
     C. toes
     D. corn

10. Mom said to stop arguing and be _____.
     A. heal
     B. trees
     C. flakes
     D. friends

Missing Words Sample Test 2

1. The hungry horse reached for the _____.
    A. happy
    B. apple
    C. rain
    D. knees

2. The nurse _____ when my uncle died.
    A. pear
    B. doctor
    C. cried
    D. thumb

3. Salmon lay their _____ in the fall.
    A. banana
    B. tomorrow
    C. sneeze
    D. eggs

4. Koala bears are _____ in Australia.
    A. smoke
    B. scoops
    C. reads
    D. found

5. The movie was supposed to _____ at one.
    A. start
    B. pencil
    C. bus
    D. actor

6. The _____ at the door had a long pole and a bucket.
    A. muddle
    B. railroad
    C. man
    D. permits

7. Why does knowledge of the weather _____ you?
    A. dream
    B. read
    C. storm
    D. help

8. Frogs make a _____ sound.
    A. sift
    B. croaking
    C. frosting
    D. green

9. She was not upset until she _____ to open the door.
    A. warm
    B. size
    C. tried
    D. eagle

10. The dirt road twisted and _____ like a pretzel.
    A. turned
    B. fish
    C. breeze
    D. orange

Missing Words Sample Test 3

1. The lungs get bigger and smaller when you _____.
   - A. shoe
   - B. breathe
   - C. hair
   - D. birthday

2. _____ get very little rain.
   - A. Bark
   - B. Teach
   - C. Skip
   - D. Deserts

3. Eagles eat small _____ up to the size of turkeys.
   - A. animals
   - B. careen
   - C. kicked
   - D. hitch

4. Dinosaurs no longer exist except in _____.
   - A. elbows
   - B. museums
   - C. fences
   - D. football

5. White light is actually _____ up of many colors.
   - A. present
   - B. sleeping
   - C. made
   - D. screech

6. An enlarged lymph ___ may be an indication of illness.
   - A. plasma
   - B. gland
   - C. grand
   - D. lump

7. The ___ from the waterfall made the nearby rocks damp
   - A. rain
   - B. splay
   - C. spray
   - D. spring

8. The lonely landscape with no trees felt ___ and cold.
     A. bleak
     B. black
     C. break
     D. warm

9. He asked her to be sincere and ___ about her feelings.
     A. jovial
     B. blue
     C. flank
     D. frank

10. It is natural to want to ___ from a dangerous situation.
     A. flee
     B. free
     C. fleet
     D. fight

Missing Words Sample Test 4

1. Our company has lost a lot of money recently and now we're in the _____.
   - A. white
   - B. blue
   - C. red
   - D. green

2. My mother just loves gardening; she has _____ fingers.
   - A. white
   - B. blue
   - C. red
   - D. green

3. When we heard the news, it came completely out of the _____.
   - A. white
   - B. blue
   - C. red
   - D. green

4. Peter is so honest; he would never tell even a _____ lie.
   - A. white
   - B. blue
   - C. red
   - D. green

5. When Jane saw Mary's new car, she was _____ with envy
   - A. white
   - B. blue
   - C. red
   - D. green

6. The opposition brought up another _____ herring during the debate yesterday.
   - A. white
   - B. blue
   - C. red
   - D. green

7. When my son came after that fight with the other boys, he was black and _____ all over.
   - A. white
   - B. blue
   - C. red
   - D. green

8. We just can't get ahead because of all this _____ tape!
    A. white
    B. blue
    C. red
    D. green

9. My opponent lacks the necessary moral _____ to be President of our great country.
    A. fibre
    B. rights
    C. hazard
    D. philosophy

10. A wolf killed three of the sheep in our _____ before he was stopped.
    A. flock
    B. lamb
    C. mutton
    D. group

Missing Words Sample Test 5

1. Don't be too severe on that child; he's very ____.
   A. lovely
   B. surprised
   C. sensitive
   D. sensible

2. He knows it's not ____ to spit on the floor.
   A. sensible
   B. wet
   C. educated
   D. polite

3. She receives an average weekly ____ of US$100.
   A. fortnight
   B. wage
   C. periodical
   D. schedule

4. It's advisable to ask someone who is ____ to judge the matter.
   A. disinterested
   B. uninterested
   C. bored
   D. dispassionate

5. The ____ in our school is to punish students caught cheating on exams.
   A. politics
   B. diversion
   C. answer
   D. policy

6. Can you ___ me 5 bucks until tomorrow ?
   A. borrow
   B. loan
   C. lend
   D. wage

7. He's been participating in competitions as a ____ for a year.
   A. ogler
   B. professional
   C. maven
   D. licensed

8. I arrived late at the conference and _____ the speaker's introductory remarks.
    A. bemused
    B. lost
    C. missed
    D. mystified

9. John and Becky _____ vows of eternal love.
    A. exchange
    B. change
    C. replace
    D. forget

10. This hotel is a top choice with fellow _____ on your selected dates.
    A. travelers
    B. hotels
    C. range
    D. selection

Verbal Relations Sample Tests

Instruction:
Following you will find ten questions. In each question you will find a pair of related words, followed by another pair in which one or both words are missing. Choose from the four options that appear after the question the word, or pair, that makes the second pair of words form the same relation as the first pair of words do.

 Available time by age:

Age	6	7	8	9	10	11	12	13
Time (Minutes)	18	15	12	12	10	10	8	8

Verbal Relations Test 1

1. Poles : Magnet | ? : Battery

A. Energy
B. Power
C. Terminals
D. Cells

2. Peace : Chaos | Creation : ?

A. Manufacture
B. Destruction
C. Build
D. Construction

3. Architect : Building | Sculptor : ?

A. Museum
B. Statue
C. Chisel
D. Stone

4. Horse : Mare | ? : ?

A.   Fox : Vixen
B.   Duck : Geese
C.   Dog : Puppy
D.   Donkey : Pony

5. Cricket : Pitch | ? : ?

A.   Ship : Dock
B.   Boat : Harbor
C.   Boxing : Ring
D.   Wrestling : Track

6. Oceans : Deserts | Waves : ?

A.   Dust
B.   Sand Dunes
C.   Ripples
D.   Sea

7. Grain : Stock | Stick : ?

A.   String
B.   Heap
C.   Collection
D.   Bundle

8. Cube : Square | Square : ?

A.   Plane
B.   Triangle
C.   Line
D.   Point

9. Bank : Money | Transport : ?

A.   Traffic
B.   Goods
C.   Speed
D.   Road

10. Fan : Wings | Wheel : ?

A.   Round
B.   Air
C.   Spokes
D.   Cars

Verbal Relations Test 2

1. Fox : Cunning | Rabbit : ?

A.   Courageous
B.   Dangerous
C.   Timid
D.   Ferocious

2. Flexible : Rigid | Confidence : ?

A.   Diffidence
B.   Indifference
C.   Cowardice
D.   Scare

3. Necklace : Adornment | ? : ?

A.   Medal : Decoration
B.   Bronze : Medal
C.   Scarf : Dress
D.   Window : House

4. Billy : Goat |

A.   Cow : Bull
B.   Lord : Maid
C.   Man : Woman
D.   Cow : Calf

5. Work : Motive |

A.   Body : Mind
B.   Wall : Paint
C.   Body : Food
D.   Petrol : Car

6. Window : Curtain |

A. Door : Frame
B. Book : Jacket
C. CPU : Cabinet
D. Casing : Wire

7. Mind : Body |

A. Water : Air
B. CPU : Hard Disk
C. Ship : Oil
D. Software : Computer

8. Mirror : Glass |

A. Music : Violin
B. Match : Matchbox
C. Shirt : Cloth
D. Air : Flow

9. Sunflower : Light |

A. Torch : Battery
B. Scholar : Books
C. Ink : Print
D. Mould : Humidity

10. Blade : Grass |

A. Dig : Shovel
B. Size : Hole
C. Grain : Rice
D. Food : Morsel

Verbal Relations Test 3

1. Enough : Excess | Sufficiency : ?

A. Adequacy
B. Surplus
C. Competency
D. Import

2. Hermit : Solitude | Intruder : ?

A. Thief
B. Privacy
C. Burglar
D. Alm

3. Skirmish : War | Disease : ?

A. Medicine
B. Patient
C. Epidemic
D. Infection

4. Skeleton : Body | Grammar : ?

A. Language
B. Sentence
C. Meaning
D. Education

5. Mature : Regressed | Varied : ?

A. Rhythmic
B. Monotonous
C. Decorous
D. Obsolete

6. Sedative : Pain | Solace : ?

A. Irritation
B. Kill
C. Grief
D. Hurt

7. Sorrow : Death | Happiness : ?

A. Love
B. Dance
C. Cry
D. Birth

8. Horse : Neigh | Jackal : ?

A. Squeak
B. Chatter
C. Howl
D. Bray

9. Ship : Sea | Camel : ?

A. Forest
B. Land
C. Mountain
D. Desert

10. Dilatory : Expeditious | Direct : ?

A. Tortuous
B. Circumlocutory
C. Straight
D. Curved

Verbal Relations Test 4

1. Pituitary : Brain | Thymus : ?

A. Larynx
B. Spinal Cord
C. Throat
D. Chest

2. Blunt : Sharp | Sow : ?

A. Water
B. Crow
C. Farm
D. Reap

3. Amnesia : Memory | Paralysis : ?

A. Movement
B. Limbs
C. Handicapped
D. Legs

4. Book : Publisher | Film : ?

A. Producer
B. Director
C. Editor
D. Writer

5. Influenza : Virus | Typhoid : ?

A. Bacillus
B. Parasite
C. Protozoa
D. Bacteria

6. Radio : Listener | Film : ?

A. Producer
B. Actor
C. Viewer
D. Director

7. Spider : Insect | Crocodile : ?

A. Reptile
B. Mammal
C. Frog
D. Carnivore

8. Foresight : Anticipation | Insomnia : ?

A. Treatment
B. Disease
C. Sleeplessness
D. Unrest

9. Virology : Virus | Semantics : ?

A. Amoeba
B. Language
C. Nature
D. Society

10. Novelty : Oldness | Newness : ?

A. Culture
B. Discovery
C. Model
D. Antiquity

Verbal Relations Test 5

1. Milk : Emulsion | Butter : ?

A. Aerosol
B. Suspension
C. Sol
D. Gel

2. Haemoglobin : Iron | Chlorophyll : ?

A. Copper
B. Magnesium
C. Cobalt
D. Calcium

3. Forecast : Future | Regret : ?

A. Present
B. Atone
C. Past
D. Sins

4. Aeroplane : Cockpit | Train : ?

A. Wagon
B. Coach
C. Compartment
D. Engine

5. Restaurant : meal | vending machine : ?

A. change
B. snack
C. candy
D. lobby

6. Coffee : cup | soup : ?

A. chicken
B. appetizer
C. bowl
D. plate

7. Melt : Liquid | Freeze : ?

A. Ice
B. Condense
C. Solid
D. Crystal

8. Tractor : Trailer | Horse : ?

A. Stable
B. Cart
C. Saddle
D. Engine

9. Flower : Bud | Plant : ?

A. Seed
B. Taste
C. Flower
D. Twig

10. Gun : Bullet | Chimney : ?

A. Ground
B. House
C. Roof
D. Smoke

Verbal Relations Test 6

1. Illiteracy : Education | Flood : ?

A.   Rain
B.   Bridge
C.   Dam
D.   River

2. Appraiser : Building | Critic : ?

A.   Book
B.   Masterpiece
C.   Judge
D.   Gold

3. Fruit : Banana | Mammal : ?

A.   Cow
B.   Snake
C.   Fish
D.   Sparrow

4. Hill : Mountain | Stream : ?

A.   River
B.   Canal
C.   Glacier
D.   Avalanche

5. Court : Justice | School : ?

A.   Teacher
B.   Student
C.   Ignorance
D.   Education

6. Command : Order | Confusion : ?

A. Discipline
B. Clarity
C. Chaos
D. Problem

7. Push : Pull | Throw : ?

A. Jump
B. Collect
C. Pick
D. Game

8. Hot : Oven | Cold : ?

A. Ice Cream
B. Air Conditioner
C. Snow
D. Refrigerator

9. Drama : Stage | Tennis : ?

A. Tournament
B. Net
C. Court
D. Racket

10. Bank : River | Coast : ?

A. Flood
B. Waves
C. Sea
D. Beach

Verbal Relations Test 7

1. Malaria : Disease | Spear : ?

A. Wound
B. Sword
C. Weapon
D. Death

2. Food : Stomach | Fuel : ?

A. Plane
B. Truck
C. Engine
D. Automobile

3. Fire : Ashes | Explosion : ?

A. Flame
B. Death
C. Sound
D. Debris

4. Ocean : Water | Glacier : ?

A. Refrigerator
B. Ice
C. Mountain
D. Cave

5. Sculptor : Statue | Poet : ?

A. Canvas
B. Pen
C. Verse
D. Chisel

6. Man : Biography | Nation : ?

A.   Leader
B.   People
C.   Geography
D.   History

7. Fog : Visibility | AIDS : ?

A.   Health
B.   Resistance
C.   Virus
D.   Death

8. Reading : Knowledge | Work : ?

A.   Experience
B.   Engagement
C.   Employment
D.   Experiment

9. Cricket : Bat | Hockey : ?

A.   Field
B.   Stick
C.   Player
D.   Ball

10. Jeopardy : Peril | Jealousy : ?

A.   Envy
B.   Insecurity
C.   Lust
D.   Sin

Verbal Relations Test 8

1. Chair : Table | ? : ?

A. Object : Prop
B. Son : Father
C. Car : Scooter
D. Pen : Paper

2. Medicine : Dose | ? : ?

A. Food : Quantity
B. Basket : Waste Paper
C. Container : Water
D. Fan : Power

3. Photograph : Film | ? : ?

A. Zero : Binary
B. Positive : Negative
C. Comma : Full stop
D. Light : Prism

4. Hardware : Software | ? : ?

A. Body : Mind
B. Paper : Colour
C. Fan : Electricity
D. Car : Scooter

5. Rectangle : Pentagone | ? : ?

A. Triangle : Rectangle
B. Diagonal : Perimeter
C. Side : Angle
D. Circle : Square

6. Convoy : Ships | ? : ?

A. Delegation: Voters
B. Deputation : Representatives
C. Politicians : Parliament
D. Boot : Saddle

7. Author : Manuscript | ? : ?

A. Optician : Spectacles
B. Engineer : Bridge
C. Architect: Blueprint
D. Doctor : Stethoscope

8. Extort : Obtain | ? : ?

A. Purify : Strain
B. Steal : Borrow
C. Explode : Ignite
D. Pilfer : Steal

9. Simmer : Boil | ? : ?

A. Glide : Drift
b. Drizzle : Downpour
c. Gambol : Play
d. Stagnate : Flow

10. Tally : Votes | ? : ?

A. Census : Population
B. Government : Laws
C. Taxation : Revenue
D. Team : Athletes

Visual Relations Sample Tests

 Instruction:
Following you will find eight questions. In each questions you will find a pair of related images, followed by another pair in which the second image is missing. Choose from the four options that appear after the question the image that completes the second pair, forming the same relation as between the first pair of images.

 Available time by age:

Age	6	7	8	9	10	11	12	13
Time (Minutes)	12	12	12	10	10	10	8	8

Visual Relations Sample Test 1

1

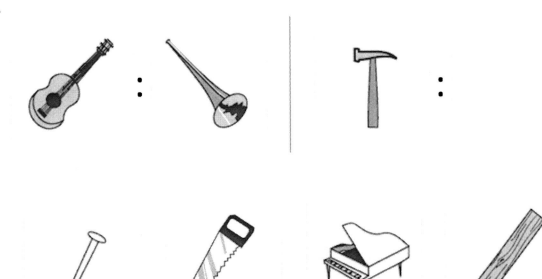

2

 :   :

A

B

C

D

3

 :     :

A

B

C

D

4

5

6

7

8

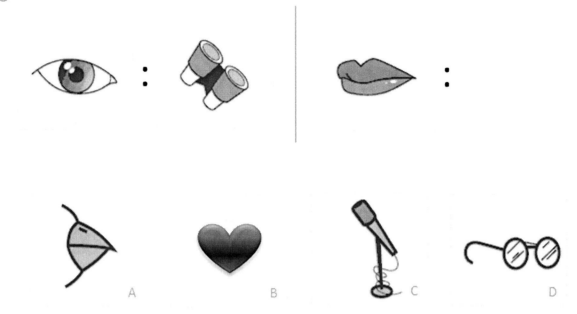

A   B   C   D

Visual Relations Sample Test 2

1

2

3

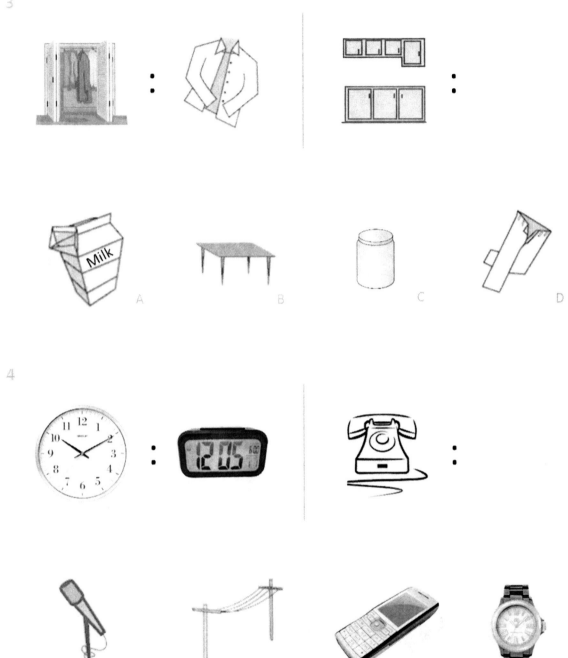

5

A	B		D

6

A	B	C	

7

8

Visual Relations Sample Test 3

1

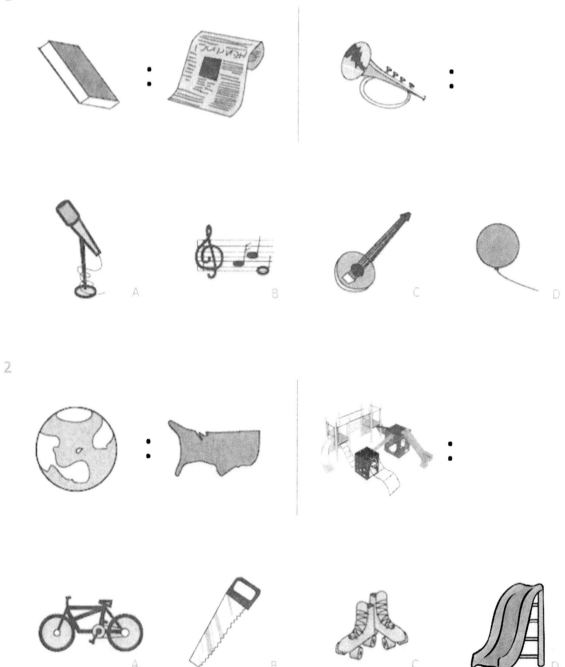

2

3

4

5

A   B   C   D

6

A   B   C   D

7

8

Visual Relations Sample Test 4

1

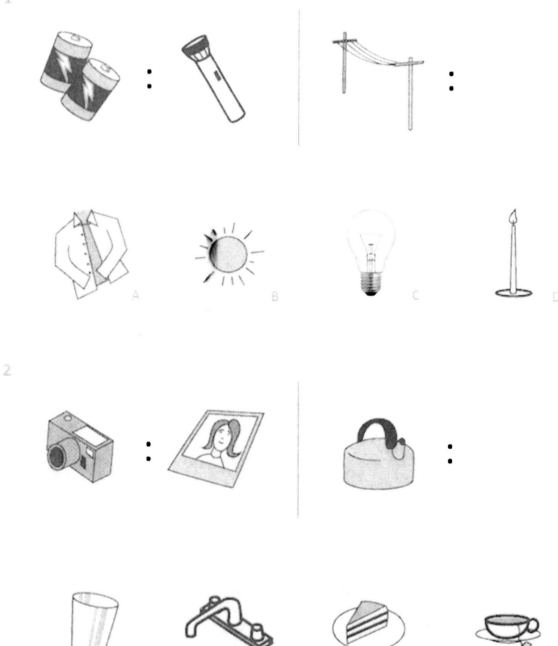

2

3

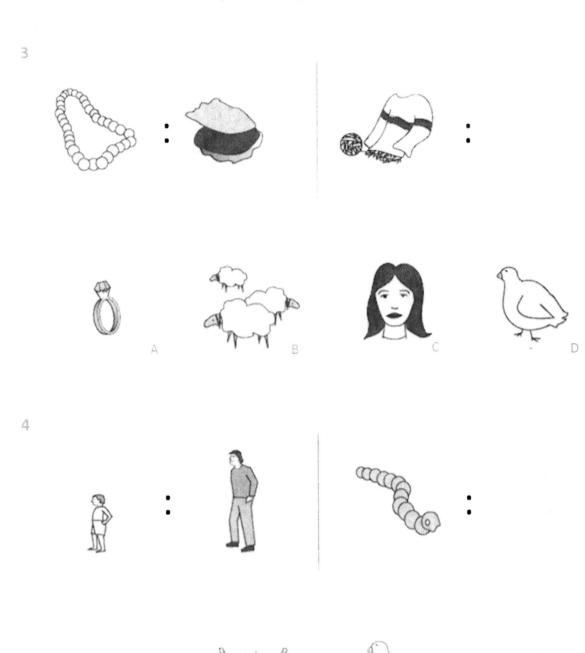

4

5

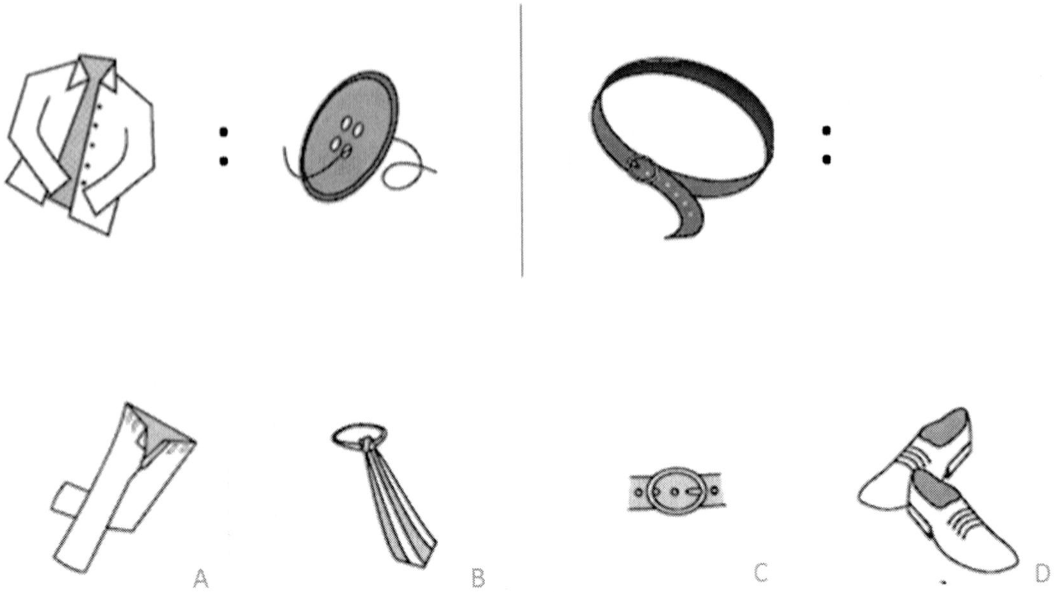

A   B   C   D

6

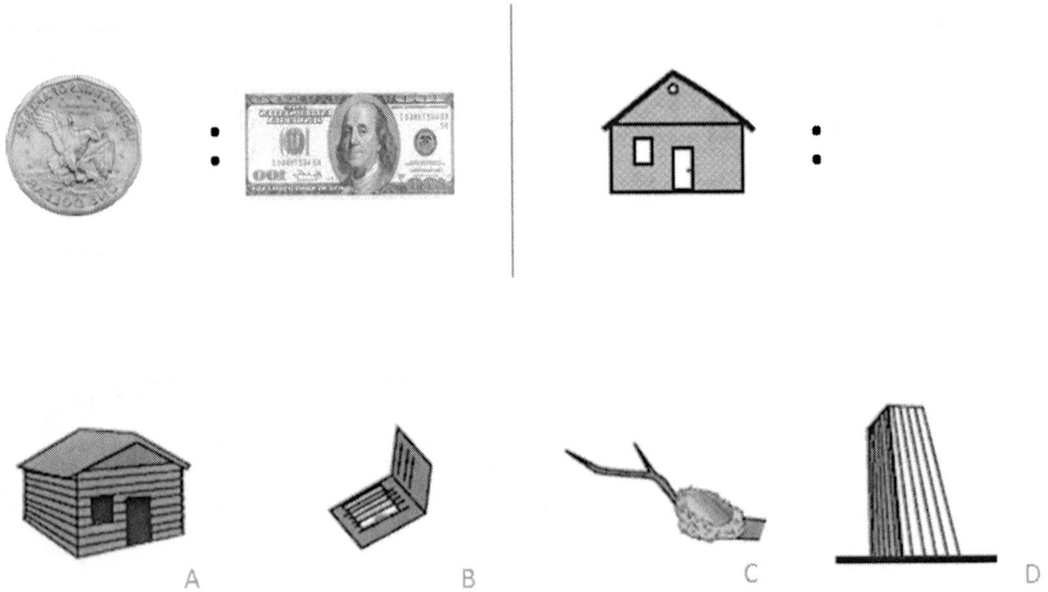

A   B   C   D

7

 :     :

A   B   C   D

8

 :    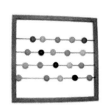 :

       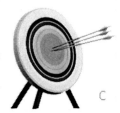   

A   B   C   D

Visual Relations Sample Test (Configurative relations)

Instruction:
Following you will find ten questions. In each question you will find a pair of related shapes, followed by another pair in which the second shape is missing. Choose from the four options that appear after the question the shape that completes the second pair, forming the same relation as between the first pair of shapes.

  Available time by age:

Age	6	7	8	9	10	11	12	13
Time (Minutes)	10	10	10	8	8	6	5	5

1

2

▭ : ▬   ◯ :

◯   ◉   ▢   ▢
A   B   C   D

3

★☆   ☆★
☆★ : ★☆   ◸◹ :
                ◺◹

◺◹   ◸◹   ◹◹   ◸◹
◸◺   ◺◺   ◺◺   ◺◸
A   B   C   D

4

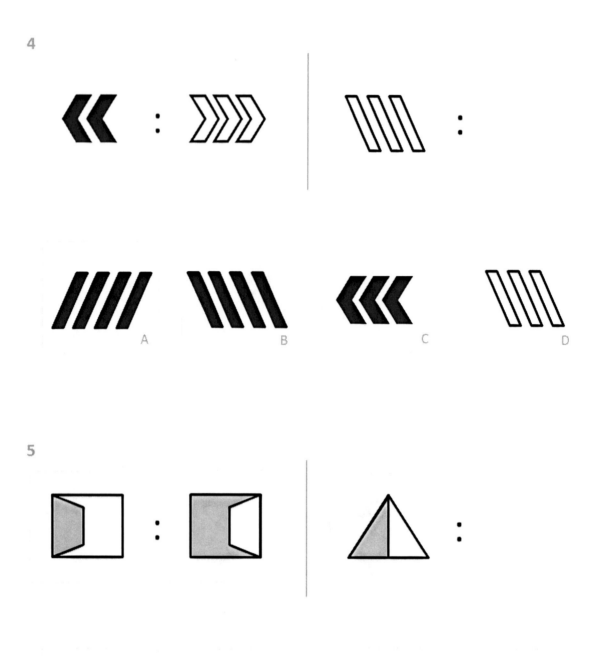

5

6

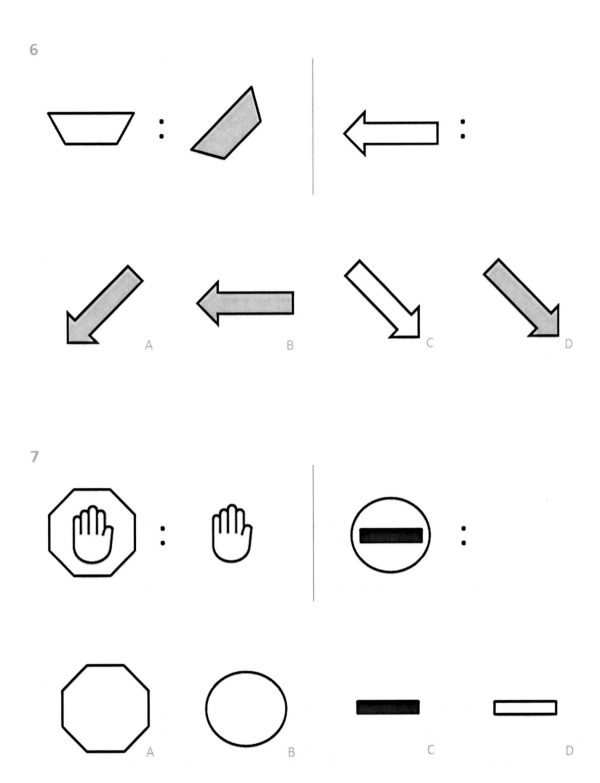

7

8

9

10

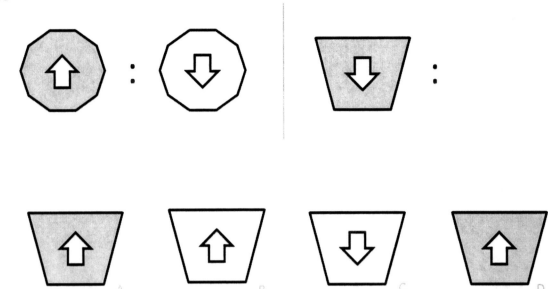

Shape Inclusion Sample Test

 Instruction:
Following you will find ten questions. In each question you will find a simple shape on the left-hand side, followed by four more complex shapes. You should select the one shape, out of the four complex shapes, that precisely includes the simple shape on the left.

 Available time by age: 5 minutes.

Age	6	7	8	9	10	11	12	13
Time (Minutes)	8	8	7	7	6	6	5	5

Shape Inclusion Sample Test 1

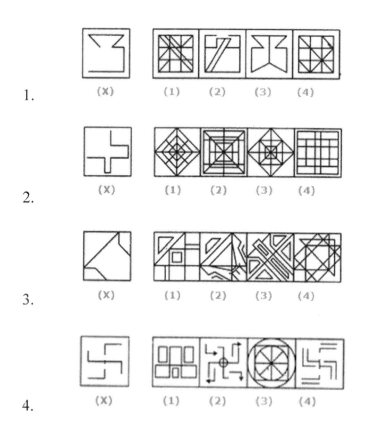

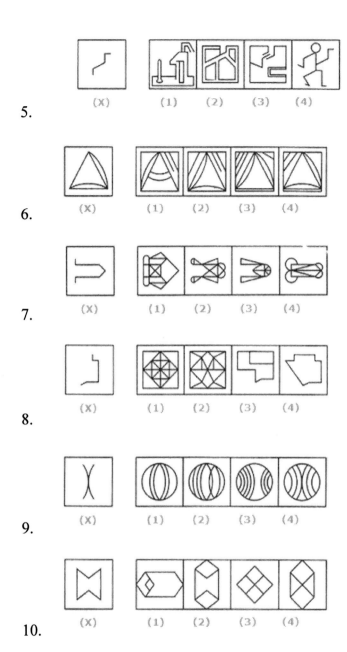

5.

6.

7.

8.

9.

10.

Shape Inclusion Sample Test 2

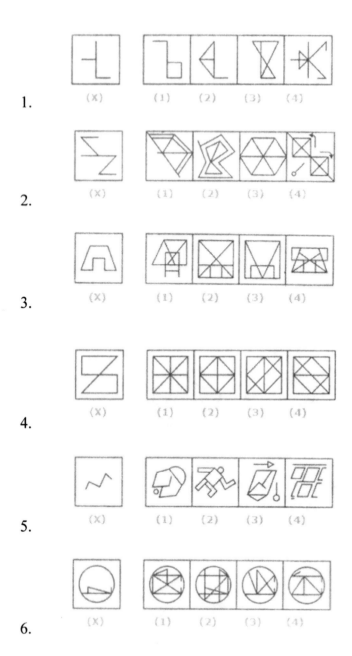

1.

2.

3.

4.

5.

6.

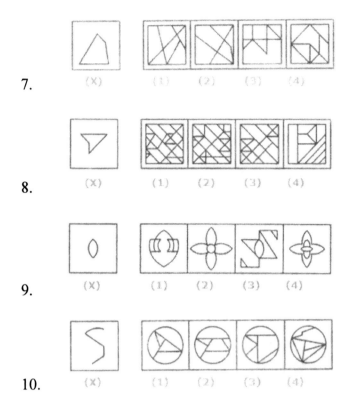

7.   (X)   (1)   (2)   (3)   (4)

8.   (X)   (1)   (2)   (3)   (4)

9.   (X)   (1)   (2)   (3)   (4)

10. (X)   (1)   (2)   (3)   (4)

Mirror Image Sample Test

Instruction:
Following you will find ten questions. In each question you will be presented with an image on the left-hand side, followed by four images. You should select the one image, out of the four options, that is the mirror image of the image on the left.

 Available time by age:

Age	6	7	8	9	10	11	12	13
Time (Minutes)	8	8	7	7	6	6	5	5

Mirror Image Sample Test 1

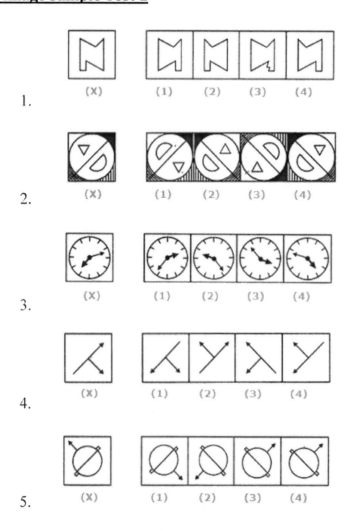

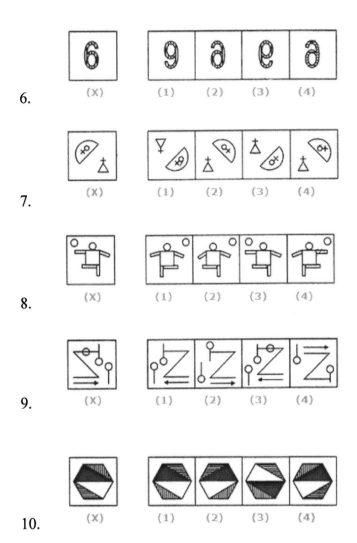

6.

7.

8.

9.

10.

Mirror Image Sample Test 2

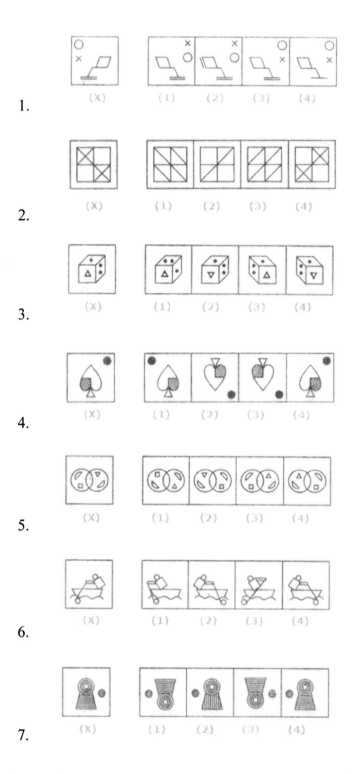

1.

2.

3.

4.

5.

6.

7.

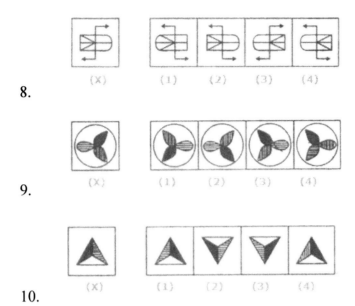

8.

9.

10.

Paper Folding Sample Test

Instruction:
Following you will find ten questions. In each question you will be presented with a pattern printed on a transparent sheet on the left-hand side, followed by four alternatives. You should select from amongst the four alternatives as to how the pattern would appear when the transparent sheet is folded at the dotted line.

 Available time by age:

Age	6	7	8	9	10	11	12	13
Time (Minutes)	8	8	7	7	6	6	5	5

Paper Folding Sample Test 1

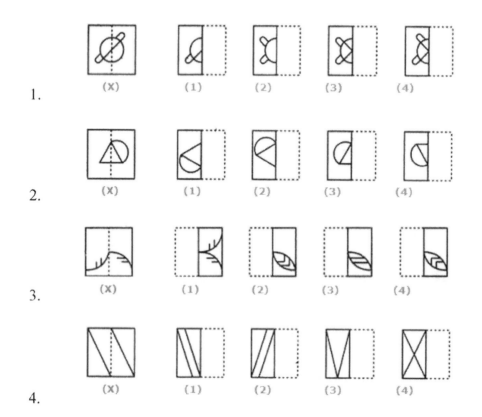

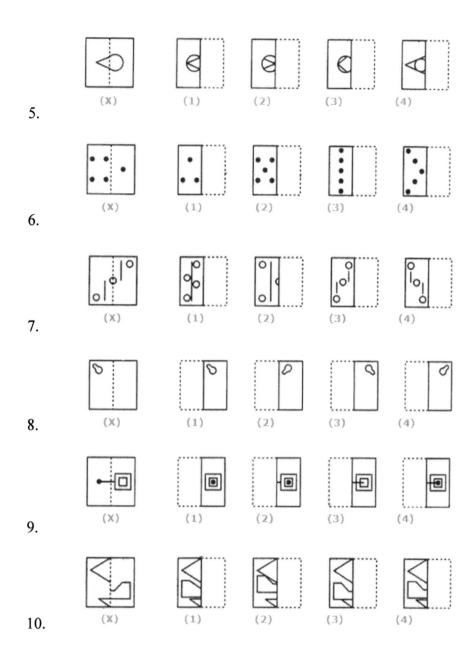

5.

6.

7.

8.

9.

10.

Sequence of Shapes Sample Tests

Instruction:
Following you will find seven questions. In each question you will find a sequence of four shapes. The fifth shape in the sequence is missing.
Choose from the four options that appear below the question the shape that best fits to continue the sequence while keeping the sequence logical and structured.

 Available time by age:

Age	6	7	8	9	10	11	12	13
Time (Minutes)	12	12	12	10	10	10	8	8

Sequence of Shapes Sample Test 1

A   B   C   D

144

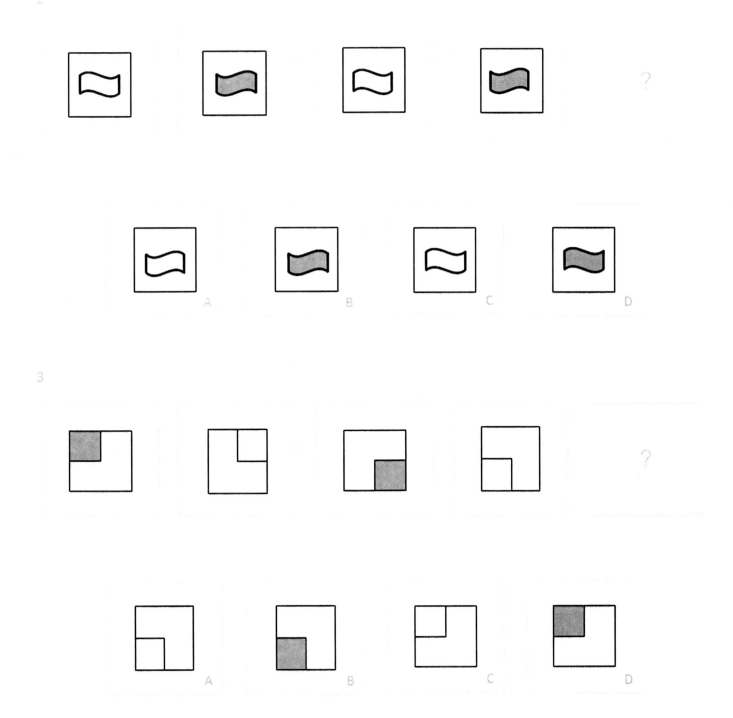

4

5

6

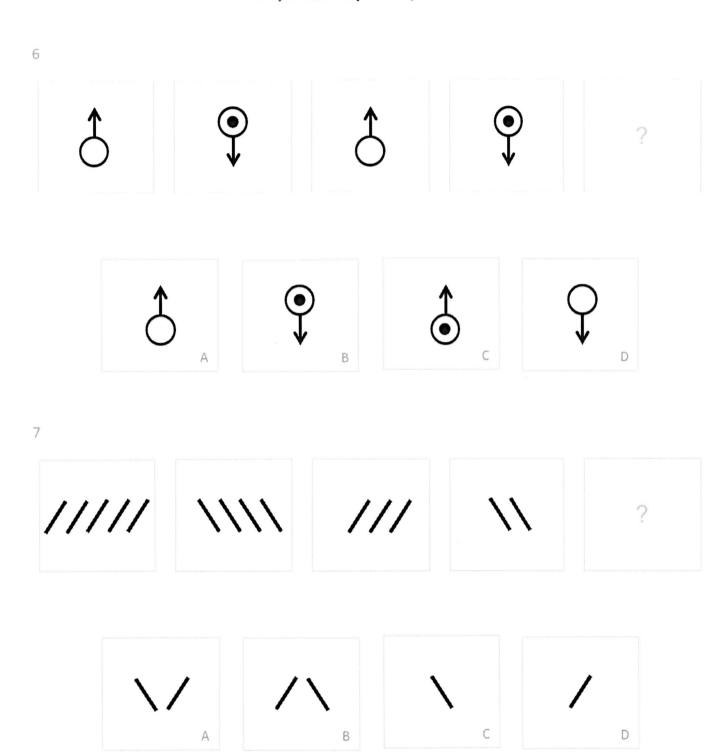

Sequence of Shapes Sample Test 2

1

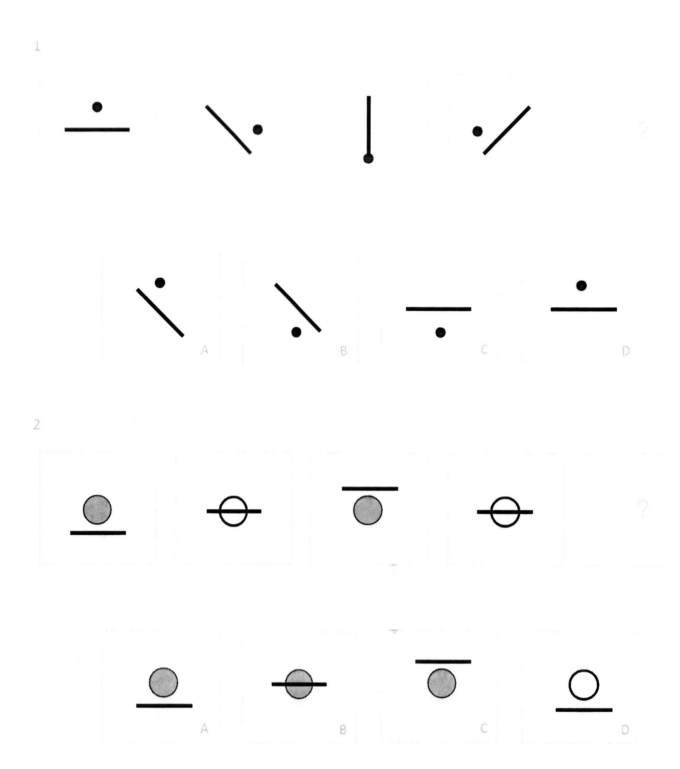

2

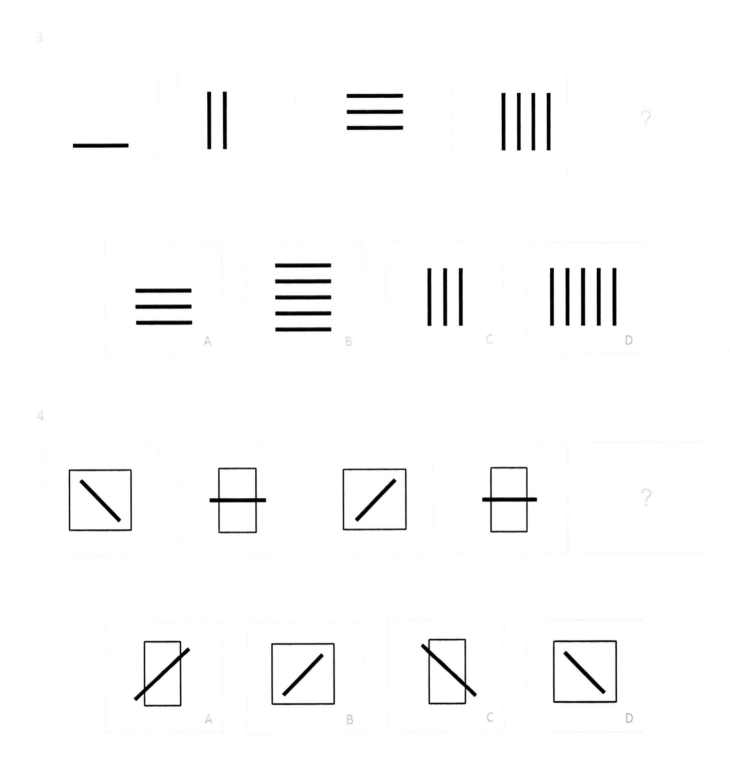

5

6

7

   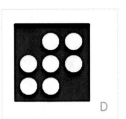

Sequence of Shapes Sample Test 3

1

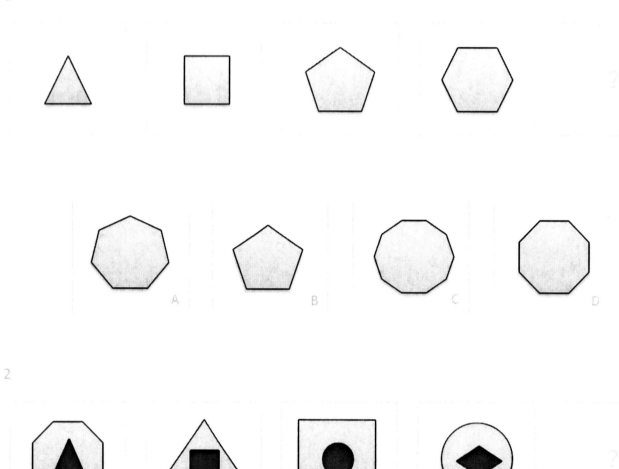

2

3

4

5

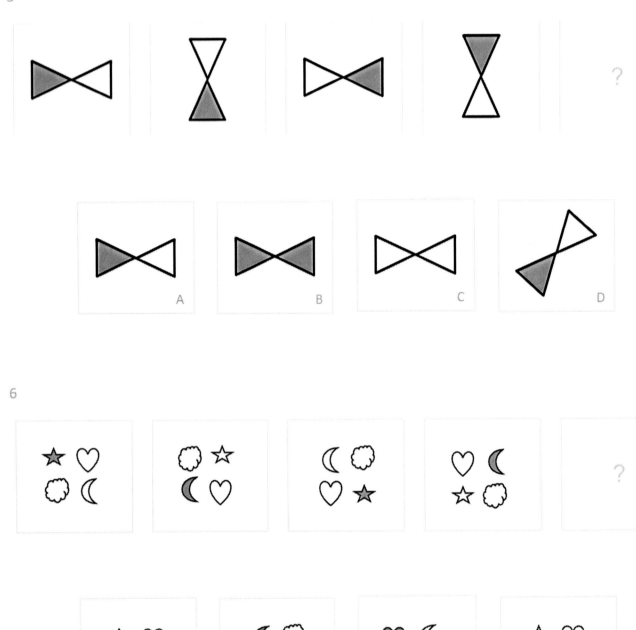

6

7

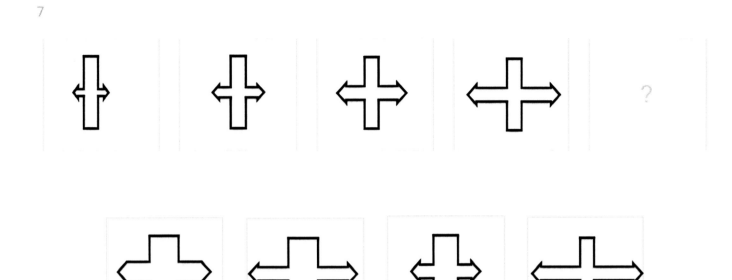

Arithmetic Word problems Sample Tests

Instruction:
Following you will find ten arithmetic word problems. Choose from the four options that appear below the right answer to the presented problem.

Available time by age:

Age	6	7	8	9	10	11	12	13
Time (Minutes)	18	16	15	15	12	12	10	8

Word Problems Test 1

1. There are 5 peaches and 47 pears in a fruit basket. How many total fruits are there in the basket?
    - a. 50
    - b. 52
    - c. 42
    - d. 48

2. Mrs. Hick used 8 pineapples and 18 apples to make fruit juice. How many fruits did she use to make juice?
    - a. 10
    - b. 20
    - c. 24
    - d. 26

3. Mr. Hurt has 49 apples and 13 pineapples for sale in his fruit shop. How many fruits is that altogether?
    - a. 62
    - b. 52
    - c. 72
    - d. 42

4. A farmer has 28 apple trees and 26 plum trees in his orchard. How many trees is that altogether?
    - a. 33
    - b. 44
    - c. 54
    - d. 55

5. Jimmy ate 4 oranges and 6 apples over the weekend. How many fruits did he eat over the weekend?
   a. 10
   b. 7
   c. 11
   d. 9

6. You have saved 47 cents last week and 50 cents this week. How many cents have you saved?
   a. 99
   b. 3
   c. 97
   d. 107

7. You visit the Toy Shop first. You buy two toys, one costing 16 cents and the other costing 19 cents. How many cents do you spend at the Toy Shop?
   a. 25
   b. 30
   c. 35
   d. 40

8. You visit the Book Shop next. You pay 21 cents for a story book and 20 cents for a book of poems. How many cents do you spend at the Book Shop?
   a. 11
   b. 21
   c. 31
   d. 41

9. You step out of your home into a long street. The Toy Shop is 21 meters to the left and the Book Shop is 20 meters to the right from your home. By how many metres are the two shops separated?
   a. 41
   b. 31
   c. 51
   d. 33

10. You return home. How many meters have you walked?
   a. 81
   b. 82
   c. 83
   d. 84

Word Problems Test 2

1. Invitations were sent to 77 relatives for a family get-together. Only 69 relatives came. How many relatives did not come?
   a. 18
   b. 8
   c. 146
   d. 156

2. Andy weighs 19 kg. His mother is 57 kg. How much more is his mother's weight (in kg)?
   a. 38
   b. 36
   c. 48
   d. 76

3. Mr. Stewart will be 38 next year. His son is 25 years younger than him. How many years old is his son at present?
   a. 10
   b. 11
   c. 12
   d. 13

4. A family party has 50 adults, 16 boys, and 17 girls. How many more adults are there at the party than children?
   a. 33
   b. 23
   c. 13
   d. 17

5. Robin is 11 years old. His aunt is 41. How many years older than him is his aunt?
   a. 42
   b. 30
   c. 32
   d. 40

The next 5 problem refers to the following text:
A mischievous monkey had collected 37 red marbles, 32 blue marbles, 14 caps, and a dozen bananas in a big bag. He decided to place 5 caps on his head and eat5 bananas. Then, while playing, he lost 11 blue marbles and 21 red marbles. He was tired and fell off to sleep. On seeing the monkey fast asleep, a fox stole the bag and ate 4 bananas.

6. How many red marbles were there in the stolen bag?
   a. 16
   b. 17
   c. 15
   d. 13

7. How many marbles were there in the stolen bag?
   a. 37
   b. 38
   c. 39
   d. 40

8. What is the maximum number of caps the fox could wear?
   a. 3
   b. 5
   c. 6
   d. 9

9. How many bananas did the fox find in the bag?
   a. 3
   b. 5
   c. 6
   d. 7

10. How many more bananas would the fox have to eat to finish all of them?
    a. 3
    b. 5
    c. 7
    d. 2

Word Problems Test 3

1. Mom had given you $5 last week. She gives you 3 times more travel money this week. How many dollars did Mom give you this week?
    a. 3
    b. 9
    c. 15
    d. 18

2. The bus ticket to Squirrel Park costs 4 times more than that to Beaver Valley. If the ticket to Beaver Valley costs $5, how many dollars is the ticket to Squirrel Park?
    a. 20
    b. 5
    c. 4
    d. 16

3. Beaver Valley is 2 miles from home. If Squirrel Park is 4 times as far, how many miles is Squirrel Park from home?
    a. 3
    b. 8
    c. 6
    d. 12

4. There are 6 men in the bus. There are 3 times more women in the bus. How many women are there in the bus?
    a. 3
    b. 12
    c. 9
    d. 18

5. You had brought home 2 flowers from Squirrel Park last time. Mom wants you to bring 5 times as many this time. How many flowers will you bring?
    a. 5
    b. 7
    c. 15
    d. 10

6. Mom had given you $15 last week. She gives you 3 times more this week. How many dollars did Mom give you this week?
    a. 15
    b. 80
    c. 30
    d. 45

7. The bus ticket costs 4 times more than what you have in your wallet. If you have only $4, how many dollars is the bus ticket?
   a. 16
   b. 12
   c. 14
   d. 18

8. An ice-cream scoop cost is $2. You asked for 4 scoop dish. How much will you pay?
   a. 8
   b. 16
   c. 32
   d. 4

9. There are 3 boys in the yard. There are 2 times more girls in the yard. How many kids are there in the yard?
   a. 2
   b. 4
   c. 6
   d. 9

10. You had bought 6 candies last time. This time you bought 5 times more. How many did you buy all together?
   a. 30
   b. 36
   c. 24
   d. 11

Word Problems Test 4

1. Barbara has $21 in her purse. Each doll costs $7. How many dolls can she buy?
    a. 3
    b. 28
    c. 14
    d. 2

2. A board game has 35 total coins. There are equal number of coins of 5 different colors. How many coins are there of each color?
    a. 7
    b. 6
    c. 5
    d. 4

3. Arthur has 14 marbles. He shares them equally among 2 friends. How many marbles does each friend get?
    a. 12
    b. 7
    c. 28
    d. 8

4. Mark has 28 blocks. He makes 7 equal stacks. How many blocks are there in each stack?
    a. 2
    b. 4
    c. 6
    d. 8

5. Diane divided 10 by 2 on her toy calculator. What quotient did the calculator display?
    a. 20
    b. 12
    c. 5
    d. 8

6. There are 10 crows perched on the branch of a tree. How many feet are there on the branch?
    a. 10
    b. 40
    c. 5
    d. 20

7. A fish tank contains 85 fish of which 7 are stationary. How many fish in the tank are moving?
   a. 68
   b. 78
   c. 88
   d. 98

8. There are 8 moths with a total of 16 white spots on their wings. If each moth has the same number of spots, how many spots on each moth?
   a. 16
   b. 8
   c. 2
   d. 144

9. There are 2 lions and 2 tigers in a circus show. How many legs are there in all?
   a. 16
   b. 14
   c. 12
   d. 18

10. A zoo has 5 African elephants and 7 Indian elephants. How many elephant's trunks are there in the zoo?
    a. 24
    b. 18
    c. 12
    d. 48

Word Problems Test 5

1. Diane loves collecting small plastic animals. She has 61 ducks and 72 goats. How many animals does she have in her collection?
    a. 133
    b. 9
    c. 144
    d. 143

2. A pond contains 75 large fish and 480 small fish. How many fish are there in the pond?
    a. 455
    b. 555
    c. 545
    d. 565

3. There are 96 doves and 818 sparrows in Shadyside Woods. How many total birds are there in Shadyside Woods?
    a. 666
    b. 718
    c. 419
    d. 914

4. There are 72 cows and 26 dogs on a farm. How many animals are there on the farm?
    a. 100
    b. 98
    c. 96
    d. 94

5. A zoo has 68 brown monkeys and 80 black monkeys. How many monkeys are there in the zoo?
    a. 148
    b. 12
    c. 158
    d. 168

6. Sarah made a necklace for her doll using 79 green beads and 31 blue beads. How many beads does the necklace have?
    a. 100
    b. 105
    c. 110
    d. 115

7. Stacy has two dolls. The first doll costs $27 and the second costs $11. How many dollars do the two dolls cost?
    a. 38
    b. 33
    c. 30
    d. 27

8. Mark empties 44 marbles from a small box into a big box that already contains 287 marbles. How many marbles are now there in the big box?
    a. 331
    b. 321
    c. 311
    d. 301

9. Arthur arranges 79 blocks in four stacks. He then arranges 144 blocks in six stacks. How many blocks did he arrange in the ten stacks?
    a. 220
    b. 221
    c. 222
    d. 223

10. Jack likes toy vehicles. He has 32 cabs and 48 vans. How many toy vehicles does he have?
    a. 70
    b. 80
    c. 90
    d. 100

Word Problems Test 6

1. Pigeons are perched on a tree. John counts 166 feet on the tree. How many pigeons are there on the tree?
    a. 332
    b. 166
    c. 342
    d. 83

2. A starfish has 5 arms. How many arms do 41 starfish have?
    a. 205
    b. 164
    c. 82
    d. 46

3. There are 83 doves and 348 sparrows in Shadyside Woods. How many total birds are there in Shadyside Woods?
    a. 431
    b. 432
    c. 433
    d. 434

4. Shadyside Forest has 699 deer. There are 391 spotted deer. How many deer do not have spots?
    a. 307
    b. 308
    c. 309
    d. 310

5. A farm has 68 hens. Each hen lays 8 eggs. How many eggs are there in all?
    a. 444
    b. 544
    c. 644
    d. 744

6. Jimmy invites 50 boys and 86 girls to his birthday party. How many friends did he invite?
    a. 126
    b. 132
    c. 136
    d. 140

7. There are 10 cakes. Each cake is cut into 6 pieces. How many pieces are there in all?
   a. 60
   b. 16
   c. 4
   d. 80

8. There are 54 sandwiches to be arranged equally in 2 trays. How many sandwiches will there be in each tray?
   a. 26
   b. 27
   c. 28
   d. 108

9. Dad has planned 50 games for the party. Each game would have 10 winners. How many prizes would Dad give away?
   a. 5
   b. 500
   c. 5000
   d. 50000

10. Mom places 20 paper plates on the table in 10 rows. How many paper plates are there in each row?
    a. 20
    b. 2000
    c. 2
    d. 200

Word Problems Test 7

1. Barbara has $160 in her purse. Each doll costs $20. How many dolls can she buy?
   a. 8
   b. 140
   c. 640
   d. 6400

2. A board game has 270 total coins. There are equal number of coins of 6 different colors. How many coins are there of each color?
   a. 90
   b. 180
   c. 45
   d. 135

3. Gary empties 26 marbles from a small box into a big box that already contains 231 marbles. How many marbles are now there in the big box?
   a. 256
   b. 257
   c. 258
   d. 259

4. Paul arranges 83 blocks in a tall stack. Accidentally, he drops 50 blocks. How many blocks are still there in the stack?
   a. 66
   b. 55
   c. 44
   d. 33

5. Cheryl multiplied 107 by 5 on her toy calculator. What product did the calculator display?
   a. 515
   b. 525
   c. 535
   d. 545

6. There are 9 flowers in a bouquet. How many flowers are there in 39 bouquets?
   a. 351
   b. 451
   c. 551
   d. 651

7. There are 48 flowers in a bunch. Each flower has 9 petals. How many petals are there in the bunch?
    a. 412
    b. 422
    c. 432
    d. 442

8. A garland has 134 roses. If 75 roses are white, how many roses are not white in color?
    a. 59
    b. 69
    c. 79
    d. 89

9. How many bunches of 7 can be made from 273 flowers?
    a. 29
    b. 33
    c. 36
    d. 39

10. A florist placed 78 gladioli equally in 13 vases. How many gladioli were placed in each vase?
    a. 5
    b. 6
    c. 7
    d. 8

Word Problems Test 8

1. Dad buys 6 train tickets for $108. How many dollars does each ticket cost?
   a. 18
   b. 19
   c. 20
   d. 21

2. The train ticket to Golden Sands costs 5 times that to Mushroom Garden. If the ticket to Golden Sands costs $125, how many dollars is the ticket to Mushroom Garden?
   a. 24
   b. 25
   c. 26
   d. 27

3. The bus stop to Beaver Valley is 110 meter from home. If the bus stop to Mushroom Garden is 5 times as far, how many meters is it from home?
   a. 500
   b. 525
   c. 550
   d. 600

4. There are 61 men in Mushroom Garden. The women are 6 times the men. How many women are there in Mushroom Garden?
   a. 355
   b. 366
   c. 377
   d. 288

5. How many women and men are there in Mushroom Garden?
   a. 864
   b. 854
   c. 844
   d. 834

6. Each section in a class has 7 students. If there are 6 sections, how many students are there in the class?
   a. 13
   b. 36
   c. 38
   d. 42

7. A class picnic is estimated to cost $77. If there are 11 children in the class, how many dollars should each child contribute?
   a. 154
   b. 28
   c. 14
   d. 7

8. If 45 children in a class are to be assigned 9 Science projects, how many children should work on each project?
   a. 4
   b. 5
   c. 6
   d. 7

9. The Math teacher does 4 sums every day. After 6 days, how many sums has she done?
   a. 22
   b. 23
   c. 24
   d. 25

10. For a school day parade, there are 5 rows with 8 boys in each row and 3 rows with 7 girls in each row. How many total students are there in the parade?
    a. 51
    b. 56
    c. 61
    d. 66

Word Problems Test 9

The next 5 problem refers to the following text:

A tailor stitches 4 shirts every day. It takes him 3 hours to stitch a shirt. Each shirt uses 6 buttons and has two pockets. Each shirt costs the tailor $ 3 and he charges the customer $5.

1. How many pockets does the tailor stitch in 34 days?
   a. 272
   b. 274
   c. 276
   d. 278

2. How many shirts does the tailor stitch if he uses 234 buttons?
   a. 37
   b. 39
   c. 41
   d. 43

3. How many dollars does the tailor collect from his customers in 7 days?
   a. 140
   b. 150
   c. 160
   d. 180

4. How many dollars does the tailor earn as profit in 15 days?
   a. 110
   b. 120
   c. 130
   d. 140

5. How many hours does the tailor work in 17 days?
   a. 204
   b. 205
   c. 207
   d. 208

6. There are 23 cakes. Each cake is cut into 9 parts. Each part is further cut into 2 pieces. How many cake pieces are there in all?
   a. 444
   b. 414
   c. 404
   d. 396

7. The Professors at the State University drank 163 cups of tea yesterday. They drank 59 cups in the morning and 60 in the afternoon. How many did they drink in the evening?
   a. 41
   b. 42
   c. 43
   d. 44

8. Gary has a collection of 111 books. He donated 19 books last year and 26 books this year. How many books does he still have?
   a. 63
   b. 64
   c. 65
   d. 66

9. A school has 5 dining halls. Each dining hall has 33 tables. If there are four children to each table, how many children stay for lunch?
   a. 440
   b. 550
   c. 660
   d. 770

10. Last month, Jack worked for 193 hours, Greg worked for 136 hours, and Edward worked 23 hours more than Jack. How many hours did they work altogether?
    a. 345
    b. 445
    c. 545
    d. 645

Word Problems Test 10
The table shows quiz marks out of 100 in each subject. The following 5 problems refer to these marks.

	English	Geography	Mathematics	Science
Robert	65	95	66	47
Samuel	63	63	86	84
Thomas	49	80	54	64

1. How many marks did Thomas totally obtain in Mathematics and Science?
    a. 115
    b. 116
    c. 117
    d. 118

2. How many more marks does Robert need for a perfect score in Mathematics?
    a. 31
    b. 32
    c. 33
    d. 34

3. In Geography, how many more marks did Robert get than Samuel?
    a. 30
    b. 31
    c. 32
    d. 33

4. Find the difference between Robert's Science marks and Samuel's English marks.
    a. 14
    b. 15
    c. 16
    d. 17

5. The Mathematics teacher by mistake gave Thomas 2 times his actual marks. What are his actual marks?
    a. 27
    b. 28
    c. 29
    d. 30

6. A school has 275 students. If they are divided into 5 sections, how many students are there in each section?
   a. 55
   b. 56
   c. 57
   d. 58

7. A class picnic is estimated to cost $300. If 15 children go for the picnic, how many dollars should each child contribute?
   a. 40
   b. 30
   c. 20
   d. 10

8. If 121 children in a school are to be assigned 11 Science projects, how many children should work on each project?
   a. 9
   b. 10
   c. 11
   d. 12

9. The Math teacher wishes to solve 279 sums. If she solves 9 sums each day, how many days will she require?
   a. 30
   b. 31
   c. 32
   d. 33

10. For a school day parade, 400 students are arranged in 8 rows. How many students are there in each row?
   a. 40
   b. 50
   c. 60
   d. 70

Series of Letters Sample Tests

 Instruction:
Following you will find ten questions. In each question you will find four sequences of letters. You should identify the exceptional series, the series that doesn't form the same sequence logic as the other three series.

 Available time by age:

Age	6	7	8	9	10	11	12	13
Time (Minutes)	18	18	15	15	12	12	10	10

Series of Letters Sample Test 1

A B C D E F G H I J K L M N O P Q R S T U V W X Y Z

1.
   - a. BCDEF
   - b. MNOPQ
   - c. KLMOP
   - d. FGHIJ

2.
   - a. PONLM
   - b. FEDCB
   - c. UTSRQ
   - d. IHGFE

3.
   - a. BBDBB
   - b. IIJII
   - c. KKMKK
   - d. QQSQQ

4.
   - a. EGIKM
   - b. BDFHJ
   - c. NPRTV
   - d. ACDFH

5.
    a. ADGJM
    b. CFILO
    c. JMPSV
    d. EGIKM

6.
    a. BCEGL
    b. DEGIN
    c. CDFHL
    d. ABDGK

7.
    a. BDBDB
    b. JLJLJ
    c. DFDFD
    d. MQNQN

8.
    a. EFEGE
    b. HJHKH
    c. ACADA
    d. FHFIF

9.
    a. IIIMI
    b. TTTVT
    c. DDDHD
    d. MMMQM

10.
    a. ABCAB
    b. DEFDE
    c. IJKIJ
    d. CDEDE

A B C D E F G H I J K L M N O P Q R S T U V W X Y Z

Series of Letters Sample Test 2

A B C D E F G H I J K L M N O P Q R S T U V W X Y Z

1.
   - a. CEGKK
   - b. DFHLL
   - c. EHJOO
   - d. BDFJJ

2.
   - a. LLLKM
   - b. BBBAC
   - c. PPPOQ
   - d. QQQRP

3.
   - a. RRQQQ
   - b. CCDDD
   - c. VVUUU
   - d. JJIII

4.
   - a. ABCBC
   - b. CDEDC
   - c. MNONM
   - d. STUTS

5.
   - a. QRSTU
   - b. NMOPQ
   - c. OPQRS
   - d. KLMNO

6.
   - a. UTSRQ
   - b. QPOMN
   - c. SRQPO
   - d. ONMLK

7.
   - a. EGEFE
   - b. HKHJH
   - c. ADACA
   - d. FIFHF

8.
      a. MKIGE
      b. JHFDB
      c. VTRPN
      d. HFDCA

9.
      a. SSSVS
      b. KKKMK
      c. GGGJG
      d. PPPSP

10.
      a. MMNOO
      b. BBCDD
      c. AABBC
      d. SSTUU

A B C D E F G H I J K L M N O P Q R S T U V W X Y Z

Numerical Series Completion Sample Tests

Instruction:
Following you will find ten questions. In each question you will find a sequence of numbers. The last number in the sequence is missing.
Choose from the four options that appear below the question the number that best fits to continue the sequence while keeping the sequence arithmetically logical.

 Available time by age:

Age	6	7	8	9	10	11	12	13
Time (Minutes)	18	18	15	15	12	10	8	8

Numerical Series Completion Sample Test 1

1. 10,20,30,40,50, ___
   a. 10
   b. 60
   c. 50
   d. 55

2. 10,30,20,40,30, ___
   a. 10
   b. 60
   c. 50
   d. 55

3. 5,8,11,14,17, ___
   a. 20
   b. 21
   c. 18
   d. 19

4. 1,3,6,8,11, ___
   a. 10
   b. 11
   c. 12
   d. 13

180

5. 11,22,33,44,__
    a. 55
    b. 45
    c. 50
    d. 43

6. 2,3,5,8,13,__
    a. 18
    b. 19
    c. 20
    d. 21

7. 60,50,40,30,20,__
    a. 30
    b. 20
    c. 10
    d. 0

8. 60,40,50,30,40,__
    a. 10
    b. 20
    c. 30
    d. 60

9. 2,4,6,10,16,__
    a. 20
    b. 22
    c. 24
    d. 26

10. 2,4,8,14,22,__
    a. 32
    b. 30
    c. 28
    d. 26

Numerical Series Completion Sample Test 2

1. 6,11,9,14,12__
    a. 13
    b. 15
    c. 17
    d. 19

2. 5,7,14,16,32,__
    a. 64
    b. 48
    c. 34
    d. 42

3. 10,8,6,4,2,__
    a. 0
    b. 1
    c. 4
    d. -2

4. 3,5,9,11,15,__
    a. 16
    b. 17
    c. 18
    d. 19

5. 1,2,3,5,8,__
    a. 11
    b. 21
    c. 9
    d. 13

6. 3,5,9,15,23,__
    a. 27
    b. 29
    c. 31
    d. 33

7. 2,4,8,16,__
    a. 20
    b. 32
    c. 24
    d. 36

8. 20,22,17,19,14,__
   - a. 18
   - b. 16
   - c. 20
   - d. 16

9. 3,6,4,7,5,__
   - a. 6
   - b. 11
   - c. 13
   - d. 8

10. 4,5,8,13,20,__
   - a. 29
   - b. 27
   - c. 25
   - d. 23

Numerical Series Completion Sample Test 3

1. 1,4,9,16,25,__
    a. 30
    b. 33
    c. 36
    d. 40

2. 12,15,16,19,20,__
    a. 21
    b. 22
    c. 23
    d. 24

3. 2,4,8,10,20,__
    a. 30
    b. 40
    c. 27
    d. 22

4. 10,5,12,7,14,__
    a. 9
    b. 16
    c. 22
    d. 30

5. 0,3,3,6,6,__
    a. 6
    b. 7
    c. 8
    d. 9

6. 3,6,12,24,__
    a. 36
    b. 40
    c. 44
    d. 48

7. 2,6,4,12,6,__
    a. 18
    b. 12
    c. 4
    d. 10

8. 4,6,10,18,34,__
    a. 40
    b. 56
    c. 60
    d. 66

9. 10,14,19,25,32,__
    a. 40
    b. 38
    c. 26
    d. 24

10. 1,2,2,4,8,__
    a. 12
    b. 18
    c. 24
    d. 32

Raven Matrices Sample Tests

Instruction:
Following you will find twelve questions. In each question you will find a matrix of elements. You should identify the pattern of shapes in each matrix, and choose from the options below the shape that best completes the matrix.

Available time by age:

Age	6	7	8	9	10	11	12	13
Time (Minutes)	24	22	20	18	16	14	12	10

Raven Matrices Sample Test 1

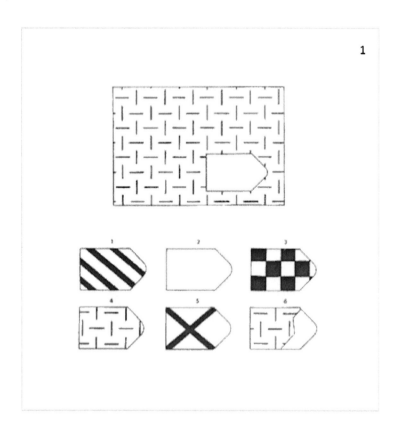

2

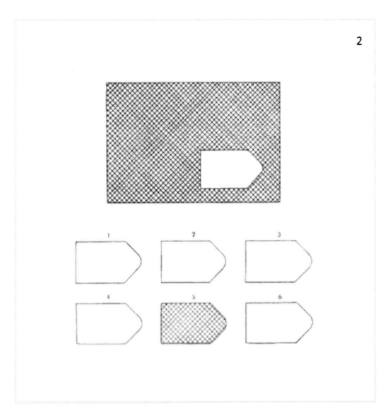

3

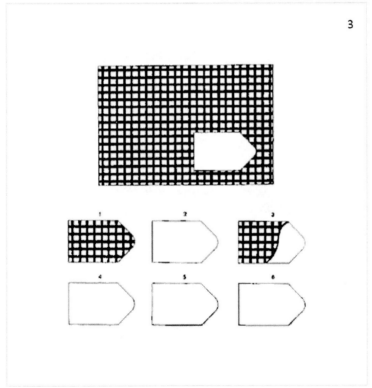

4

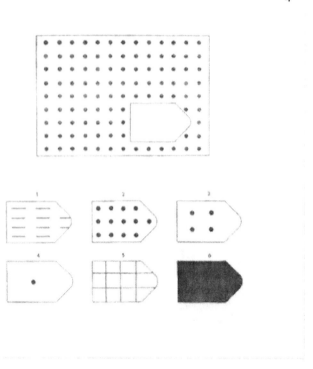

5

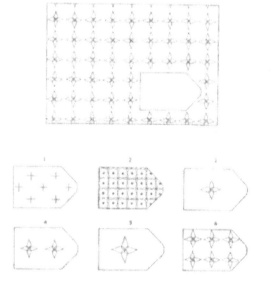

6

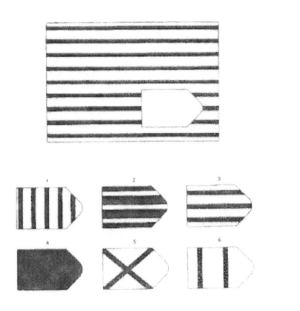

7

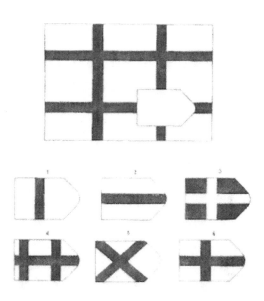

8

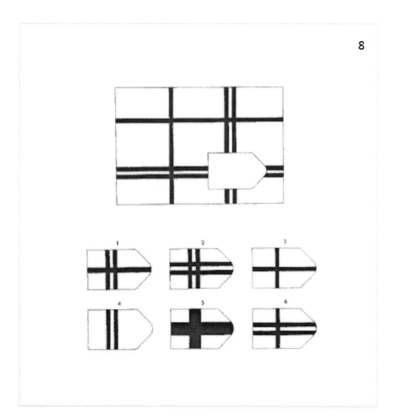

9

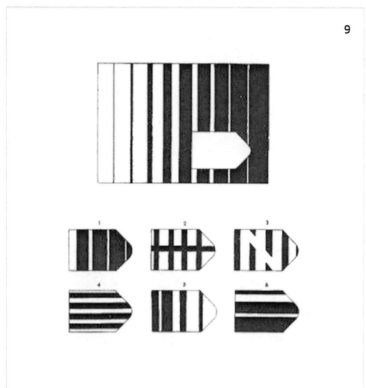

10

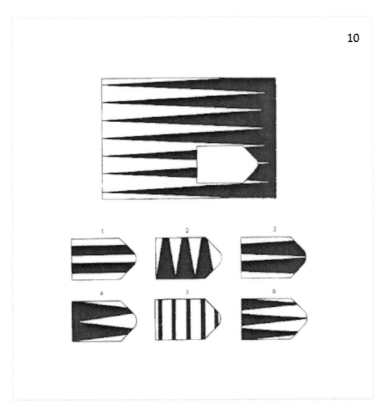

11

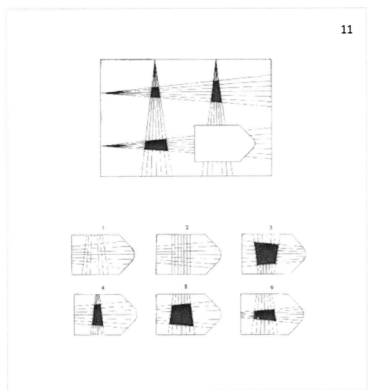

12

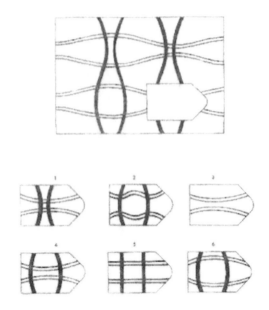

Raven Matrices Sample Test 2

1

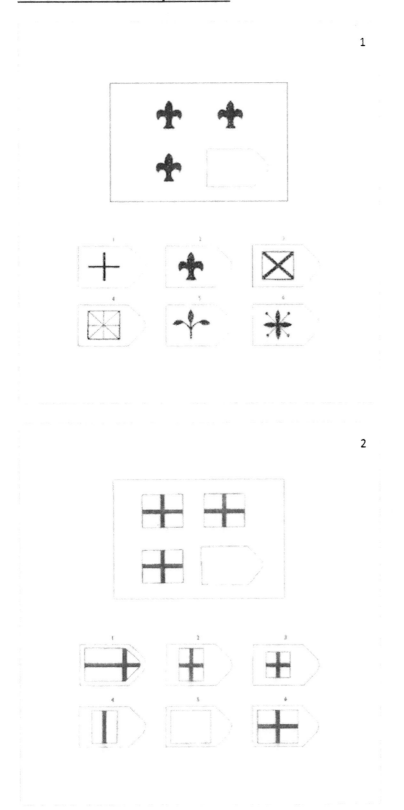

2

3

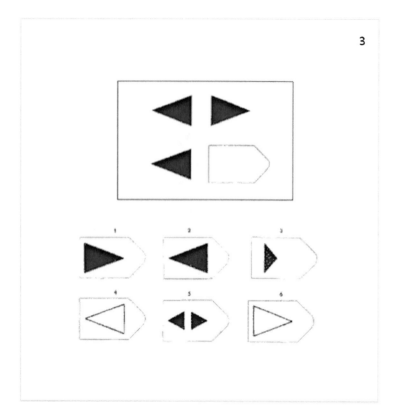

4

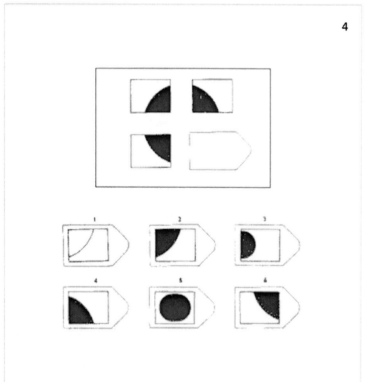

5

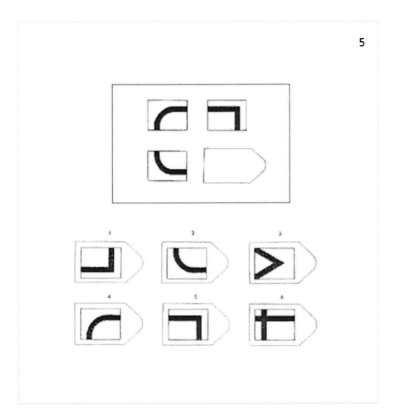

6

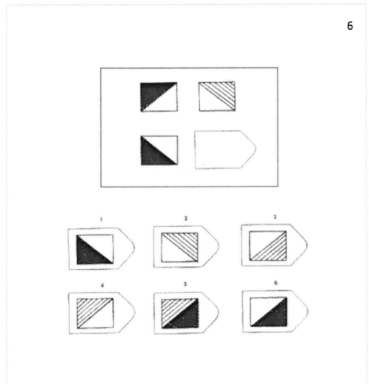

7

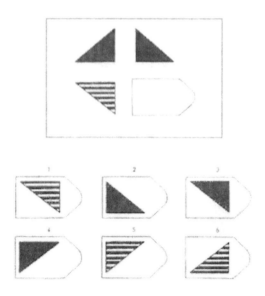

8

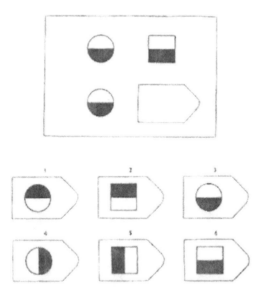

9

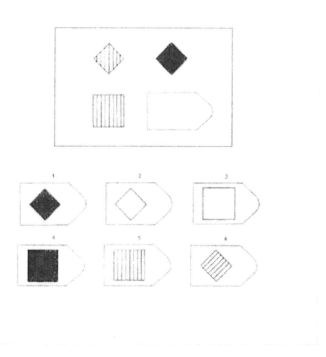

10

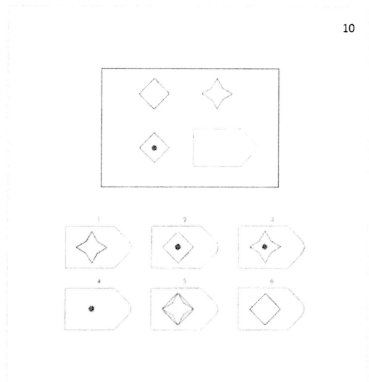

11

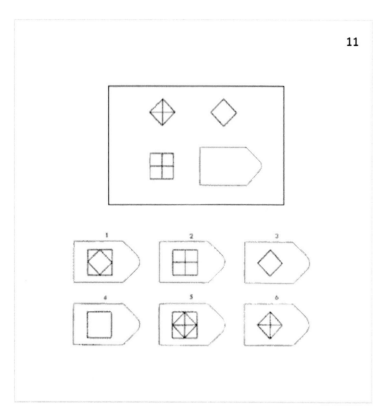

12

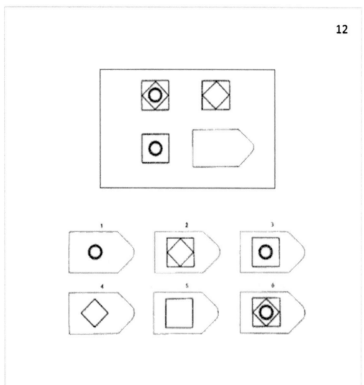

Raven Matrices Sample Test 3

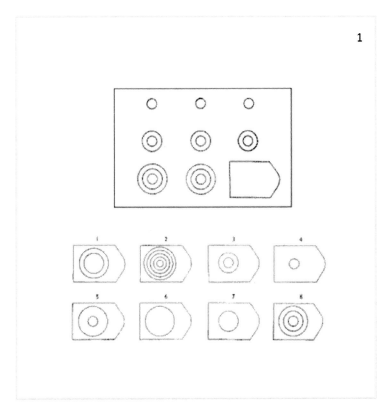

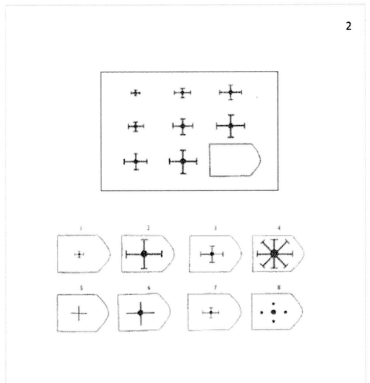

3

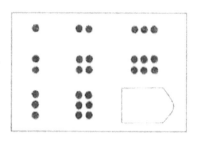

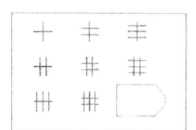

4

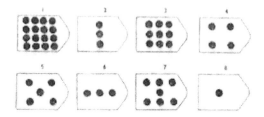

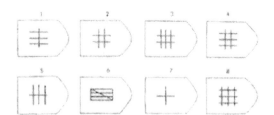

5

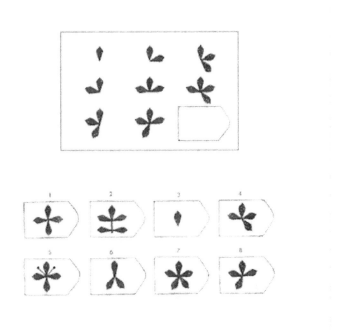

6

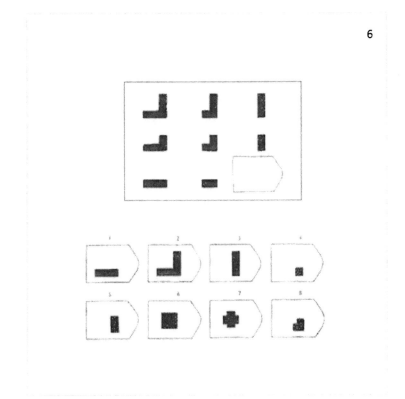

Get your child ready for an IQ test

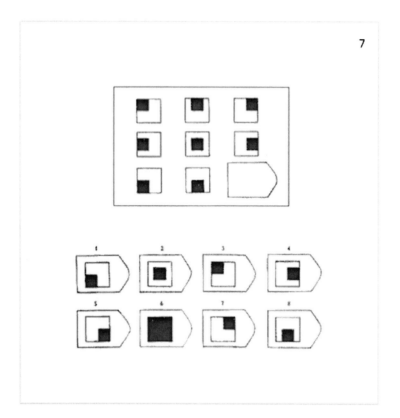

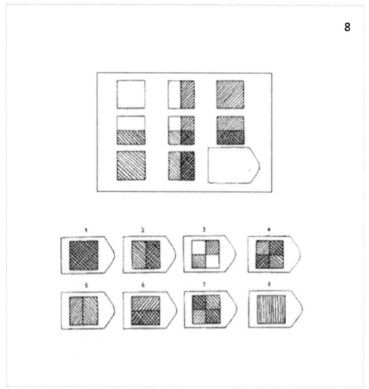

9

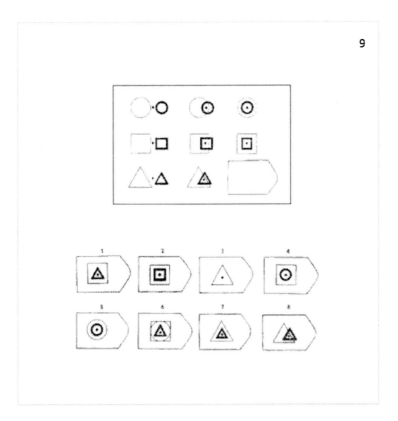

10

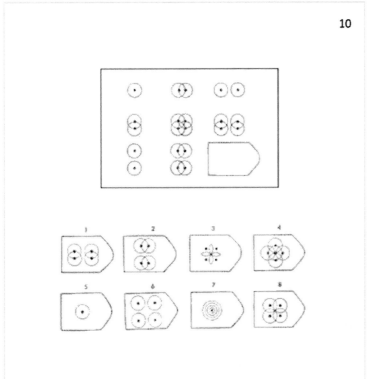

11

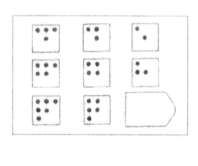

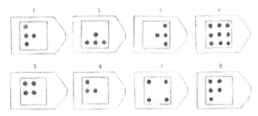

12

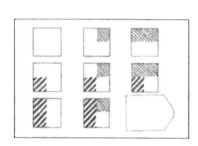

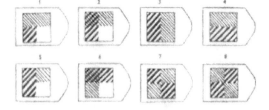

Raven Matrices Sample Test 4

1

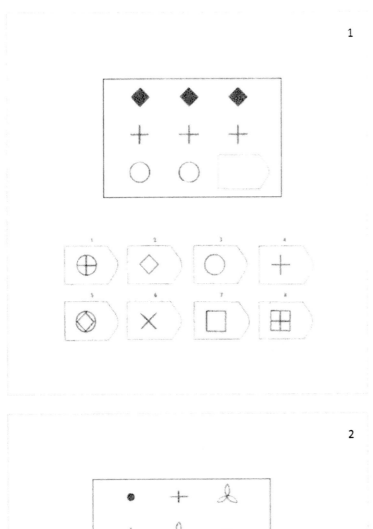

2

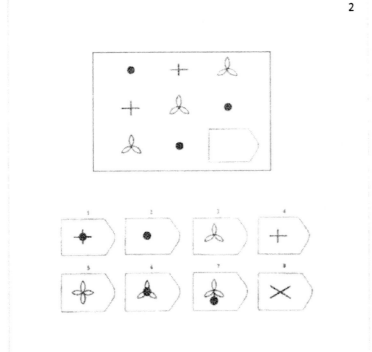

3

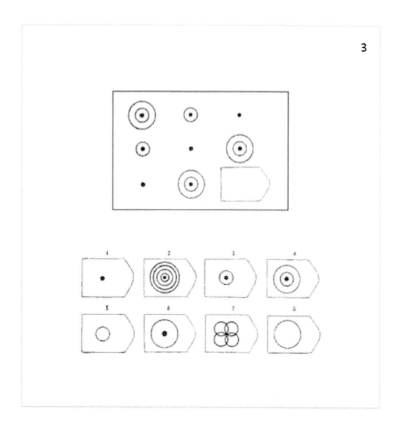

4

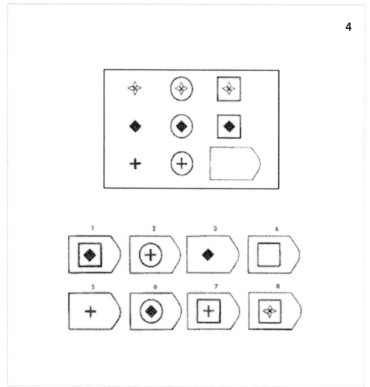

5

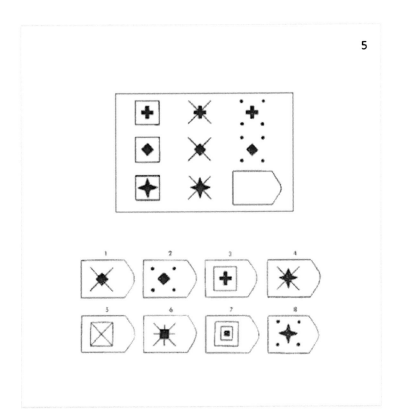

6

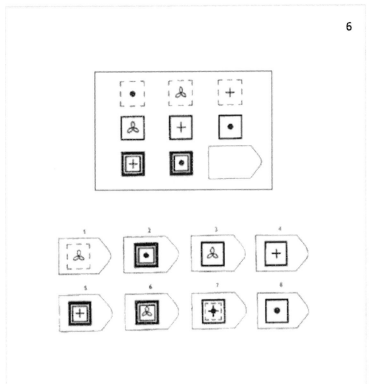

7

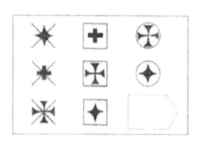

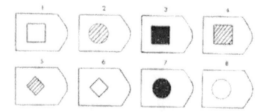

8

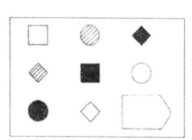

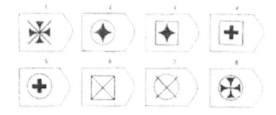

9

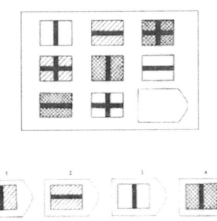

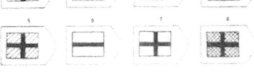

10

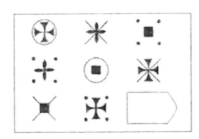

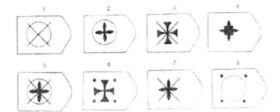

11

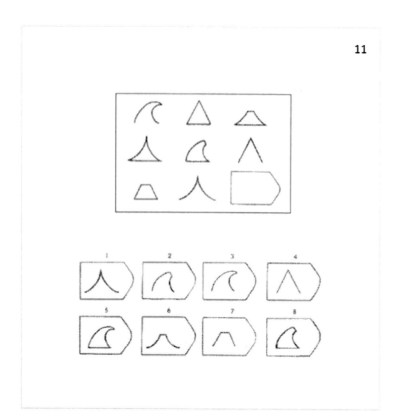

12

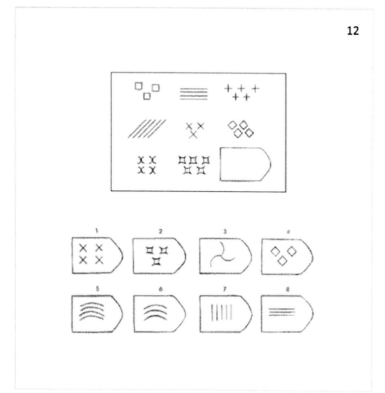

Raven Matrices Sample Test 5

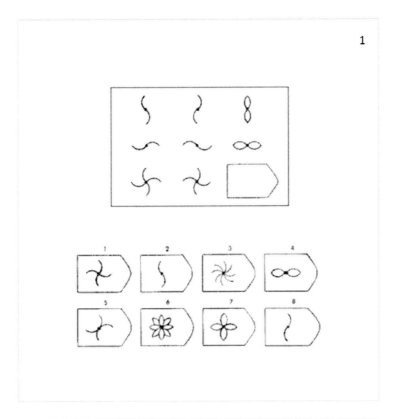

3

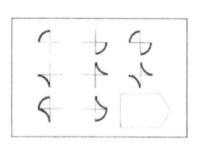

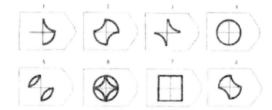

4

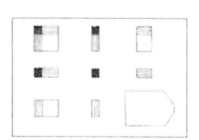

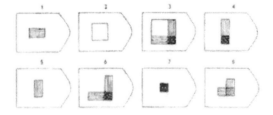

5

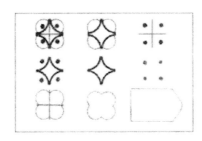

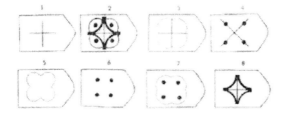

6

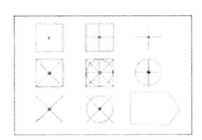

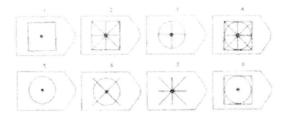

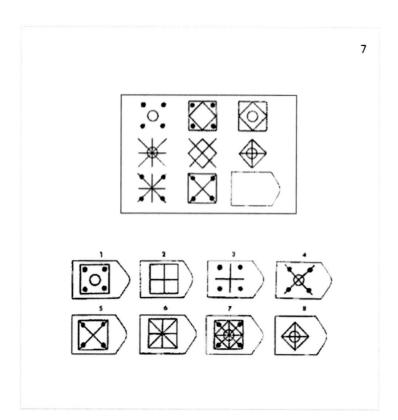

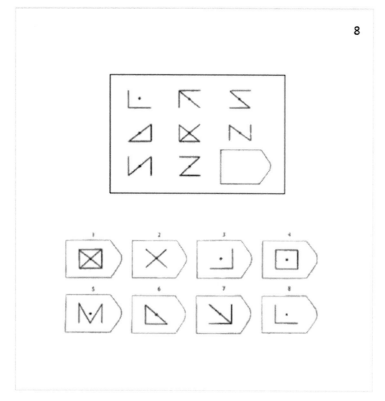

9

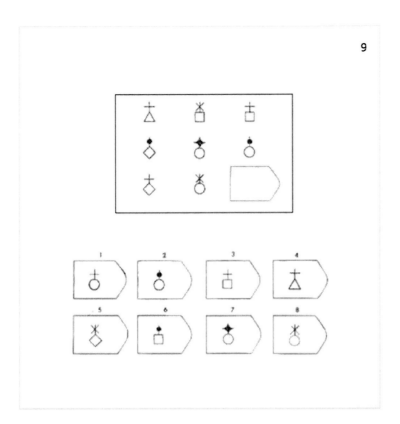

10

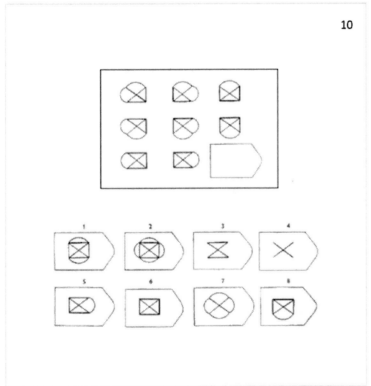

11

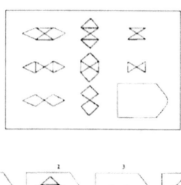

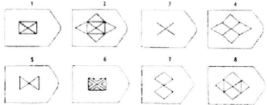

12

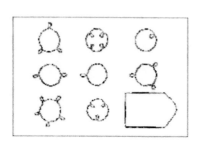

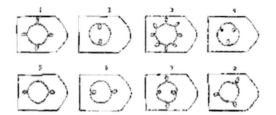

Answers

General Knowledge Sample Tests Answers

<u>Test 1</u>
1. B
2. B
3. A
4. D
5. A
6. C
7. B
8. C
9. A
10. D

<u>Test 2</u>
1. A
2. B
3. D
4. B
5. B
6. A
7. D
8. C
9. A
10. B

<u>Test 3</u>
1. A
2. B
3. A
4. B
5. A
6. D
7. C
8. A
9. B
10. B

Test 4

1. A
2. C
3. A
4. D
5. B
6. C
7. C
8. D
9. B
10. A

Test 5

1. C
2. B
3. C
4. D
5. B
6. B
7. D
8. C
9. C
10. C

Test 6

1. A
2. B
3. B
4. A
5. D
6. A
7. C
8. A
9. C
10. B

Test 7

1. A
2. D
3. B
4. A
5. B
6. C
7. A
8. B
9. D
10. C

Test 8

1. B
2. B
3. B
4. A
5. B
6. C
7. A
8. A
9. C
10. D

Test 9

1. A
2. C
3. A
4. A
5. D
6. A
7. A
8. A
9. B
10. D

Test 10

1. D
2. C
3. C
4. D
5. B
6. A
7. B
8. A
9. A
10. D

Test 11

1. A
2. A
3. D
4. D
5. A
6. A
7. B
8. B
9. A
10. D

Test 12

1. C
2. D
3. C
4. D
5. C
6. C
7. B
8. D
9. A
10. C

Synonyms Sample Tests Answers

Test 1

1. B
2. D
3. A
4. B
5. D
6. C
7. D
8. D
9. C
10. D

Test 2

1. C
2. B
3. A
4. C
5. B
6. D
7. C
8. B
9. A
10. A

Test 3

1. D
2. D
3. C
4. A
5. B
6. C
7. C
8. B
9. D
10. B

Test 4

1. D
2. C
3. D
4. B
5. A
6. B
7. B
8. C
9. D
10. D

Test 5

1. D
2. B
3. D
4. B
5. A
6. B
7. D
8. D
9. D
10. A

Test 6

1. C
2. D
3. D
4. D
5. D
6. C
7. B
8. A
9. D
10. C

Test 7

1. D
2. B
3. C
4. D
5. C
6. D
7. C
8. C
9. D
10. B

Test 8

1. B
2. C
3. C
4. B
5. D
6. B
7. A
8. D
9. C (B is also a valid answer)
10. D

Antonyms Sample Tests Answers

Test 1

1. C
2. B
3. D
4. C
5. B
6. A
7. A
8. D
9. B
10. C

Test 2

1. A
2. B
3. C
4. D
5. B
6. D
7. B
8. C
9. A
10. C

Test 3

1. A
2. A
3. D
4. B
5. C
6. B
7. A
8. D
9. B
10. C

Test 4

1. D
2. B
3. C
4. A
5. D
6. C
7. B
8. A
9. B
10. C

Test 5

1. A
2. B
3. C
4. B
5. A
6. D
7. D
8. A
9. B
10. C

Test 6

1. B
2. C
3. B
4. A
5. D
6. D
7. D
8. A
9. D
10. C

Test 7

1. D
2. D
3. A
4. B
5. C
6. D
7. A
8. B
9. C
10. D

Test 8

1. A
2. B
3. C
4. B
5. C
6. A
7. D
8. E
9. E
10. D

Odd One Out Sample Tests Answers

Test 1

1. D
2. A
3. D
4. D
5. A
6. C
7. A
8. C
9. A
10. D

Test 2

1. B
2. D
3. C
4. A
5. C
6. D
7. C
8. C
9. C
10. D

Test 3

1. B
2. C
3. A
4. C
5. D
6. A
7. C
8. A
9. D
10. C

Test 4

1. A
2. C
3. C
4. C
5. B
6. D
7. B
8. C
9. A
10. D (All the others are palindrome: reads the same backward or forward)

Test 5

1. A
2. B
3. C
4. B
5. A
6. C
7. B
8. A
9. A
10. B

Missing Words Sample Tests Answers

Test 1

1. D
2. B
3. C
4. A
5. B
6. D
7. C
8. C
9. A
10. D

Test 2

1. B
2. C
3. D
4. D
5. A
6. C
7. D
8. B
9. C
10. A

Test 3

1. B
2. D
3. A
4. B
5. C
6. B
7. C
8. A
9. D
10. A

Test 4

1. C
2. D
3. B
4. A
5. D
6. C
7. B
8. C
9. A
10. A

Test 5

1. C
2. D
3. B
4. A
5. D
6. C
7. B
8. C
9. A
10. A

Verbal Relations Sample Tests Answers

Test 1

1. C.
2. B.
3. D.
4. A.
5. C.
6. B.
7. D.
8. C.
9. B.
10. C.

Test 2

1. A.
2. A.
3. A.
4. C.
5. D.
6. C.
7. D.
8. C.
9. B.
10. C.

Test 3

1. B.
2. C.
3. C.
4. A.
5. B.
6. C.
7. D.
8. C.
9. D.
10. B.

Test 4

1. D.
2. D.
3. A.
4. A.
5. D.
6. C.
7. A.
8. C.
9. B.
10. D.

Test 5

1. D.
2. B.
3. C.
4. D.
5. B.
6. C.
7. C.
8. B.
9. A.
10. D.

Test 6

1. C.
2. A.
3. A.
4. A.
5. D.
6. C.
7. C.
8. D.
9. C.
10. C.

Test 7

1. C.
2. C.
3. D.
4. B.
5. C.
6. D.
7. B.
8. A.
9. B.
10. A.

Test 8

1. D.
2. A.
3. A.
4. A.
5. A.
6. B.
7. C.
8. D.
9. B.
10. A.

Visual Relations Sample Tests Answers

Test 1

1. B
2. D
3. D
4. C
5. B
6. A
7. B
8. C

Test 2

1. A
2. B
3. C
4. C
5. A
6. A
7. A
8. A

Test 3

1. C
2. D
3. A
4. C
5. D
6. B
7. A
8. C

Test 4

1. C
2. D
3. B
4. B
5. C (A can also be considered a correct answer, although C is more accurate)
6. D
7. D
8. C

Test 5 (Configurative Relations)

1. D
2. C
3. D
4. B
5. A
6. A
7. C
8. C
9. A
10. B

Shape Inclusion Sample Test Answers

Test 1

1. 1
2. 4
3. 4
4. 3
5. 4
6. 4
7. 2
8. 4
9. 4
10. 2

Test 2

1. 2
2. 4
3. 4
4. 1
5. 2
6. 2
7. 2
8. 1
9. 3
10. 2

Mirror Image Sample Tests Answers

Test 1

1. 4
2. 4
3. 4
4. 3
5. 3
6. 2
7. 2
8. 4
9. 3
10. 4

Test 2

1. 3
2. 4
3. 3
4. 1
5. 2
6. 4
7. 4
8. 4
9. 3
10. 1

Paper Folding Sample Test Answers

Test 1

1. 4
2. 3
3. 4
4. 4
5. 1
6. 2
7. 2
8. 4
9. 4
10. 3

Sequence of Shapes Sample Tests Answers

Test 1

1. D
2. C
3. D
4. C
5. B
6. A
7. D

Test 2

1. D
2. A
3. B
4. D
5. A
6. D
7. C

Test 3

1. A
2. C
3. C
4. D
5. A
6. A
7. D

Arithmetic Word problems Sample Tests Answers

Test 1

1. B
2. D
3. A
4. C
5. A
6. C
7. C
8. D
9. A
10. B

Test 2

1. B
2. A
3. C
4. D
5. B
6. A
7. A
8. D
9. D
10. A

Test 3

1. C
2. A
3. B
4. D
5. D
6. D
7. A
8. A
9. C
10. B

Test 4

1. A
2. A
3. B
4. B
5. C
6. D
7. B
8. C
9. A
10. C

Test 5

1. A
2. B
3. D
4. B
5. A
6. C
7. A
8. A
9. D
10. B

Test 6

1. D
2. A
3. A
4. B
5. B
6. C
7. A
8. B
9. A
10. D

Test 7

1. A
2. C
3. B
4. D
5. C
6. A
7. C
8. A
9. D
10. B

Test 8

1. A
2. B
3. C
4. B
5. A
6. D
7. D
8. B
9. C
10. C

Test 9

1. A
2. B
3. A
4. B
5. A
6. B
7. D
8. D
9. C
10. C

Test 10

1. D
2. D
3. C
4. C
5. A
6. A
7. C
8. C
9. B
10. B

Series of Letters Sample Tests Answers

Test 1

1. c. KLMOP
2. a. PONLM
3. b. IIJII
4. d. ACDFH
5. d. EGIKM
6. c. CDFHL
7. d. MQNQN
8. a. EFEGE
9. b. TTTVT
10. a. ABCAB

Test 2

1. c. EHJOO
2. d. QQQRP
3. b. CCDDD
4. a. ABCBC
5. b. NMOPQ
6. b. QPOMN
7. a. EGEFE
8. d. HFDCA
9. b. KKKMK
10. c. AABBC

Numerical Series Completion Sample Tests Answers

Test 1

1. 10,20,30,40,50, __
   b. 60

2. 10,30,20,40,30, __
   c. 50

3. 5,8,11,14,17, __
   a. 20

4. 1,3,6,8,11, __
   d. 13

5. 11,22,33,44, __
   a. 55

6. 2,3,5,8,13, __
   d. 21

7. 60,50,40,30,20, __
   c. 10

8. 60,40,50,30,40, __
   b. 20

9. 2,4,6,10,16, __
   d. 26

10. 2,4,8,14,22, __
    a. 32

Test 2

1. 6,11,9,14,12___
   c. 17

2. 5,7,14,16,32,___
   c. 34

3. 10,8,6,4,2,___
   a. 0

4. 3,5,9,11,15,___
   b. 17

5. 1,2,3,5,8,___
   d. 13

6. 3,5,9,15,23,___
   d. 33

7. 2,4,8,16,___
   b. 32

8. 20,22,17,19,14,___
   b. 16

9. 3,6,4,7,5,___
   d. 8

10. 4,5,8,13,20,___
    a. 29

Test 3

1. 1,4,9,16,25,___
   c. 36

2. 12,15,16,19,20,___
   c. 23

3. 2,4,8,10,20,___
   d. 22

4. 10,5,12,7,14,___
   a. 9

5. 0,3,3,6,6,___
   d. 9

6. 3,6,12,24,___
   d. 48

7. 2,6,4,12,6,___
   a. 18

8. 4,6,10,18,34,___
   d. 66

9. 10,14,19,25,32,___
   a. 40

10. 1,2,2,4,8,___
    d. 32

Raven Matrices Sample Tests Answers

Test 1

1. 4
2. 5
3. 1
4. 2
5. 6
6. 3
7. 6
8. 2
9. 1
10. 3
11. 1
12. 4

Test 2

1. 2
2. 6
3. 1
4. 2
5. 1
6. 3
7. 5
8. 6
9. 4
10. 3
11. 4
12. 5

Test 3

1. 8
2. 2
3. 3
4. 8
5. 7
6. 4
7. 5
8. 1
9. 7
10. 6
11. 1
12. 2

Test 4

1. 3
2. 4
3. 3
4. 7
5. 8
6. 6
7. 5
8. 4
9. 1
10. 2
11. 5
12. 6

Test 5

1. 7
2. 6
3. 8
4. 2
5. 1
6. 5
7. 2
8. 4
9. 1
10. 6
11. 3
12. 5

The End

.

CPSIA information can be obtained at www.ICGtesting.com
Printed in the USA
LVOW09s1824211016

509751LV00007B/404/P

9 781514 853719